DOCUMENTS OF MODERN HISTORY

General Editor: A. G. Dickens

John Calvin

G. R. Potter and M. Greengrass

St. Martin's Press
New York

ISBN 0-312-44277-7.

Library of Congress Cataloging in Publication Data

Potter, George Richard, 1900-
  John Calvin.

  (Documents of modern history)
  Bibliography: p.
  Includes index.
  1. Calvin, Jean, 1509-1564. 2. Reformation—
Biography. I. Greengrass, M. II. Title.
BX9418.P66   1983   284′.2′0924 [B]   82-23088
ISBN 0-312-44277-7

Contents

x

Abbreviations and Note on Translations

Battles and Hugo	J. Calvin, *Commentary on Seneca's De Clementia*, ed. F.L. Battles and A.M. Hugo (Leiden, 1969)
Beza	*Histoire ecclésiastique des églises réformées au royaume de France* (attributed to Theodore Beza) (Antwerp, 1580)
CR	*Corpus Reformatorum (Opera Calvini)*, ed. G. Baum, E. Cunitz, and E. Reuss (59 vols., Brunswick, 1863–80)
Daniel	J. Calvin, *Commentaries on the Book of the Prophet Daniel*, trans. and ed. T. Myers (2 vols., Edinburgh, 1852–3)
Ephesians	J. Calvin, *Sermons on the Epistle to the Ephesians* (Edinburgh, 1973)
Galations	J. Calvin, *Commentaries on the Epistles of Paul to the Galations and Ephesians*, trans. W. Pringle (Edinburgh, 1854)
Gospel Harmony	J. Calvin, *Commentaries on A Harmony of the Gospels, Matthew, Mark and Luke* trans. A.W. Morrison (3 vols., Edinburgh, 1922)
Institutes	J. Calvin, *The Institutes of the Christian Religion*, trans. F.L. Battles, ed. J.T. McNeill (2 vols., *Library of the Christian Classics*, Philadelphia, 1961)

Isaiah	J. Calvin, *Commentaries on The Book of the Prophet Isaiah*, trans. W. Pringle (4 vols., Edinburgh, 1850–3)
Jeremiah	J. Calvin, *Commentaries on The Book of the Prophet Jeremiah and the Lamentations*, trans. J. Owen (5 vols., Edinburgh, 1850–5)
Minor Prophets	J. Calvin, *Commentaries on the Twelve Minor Prophets*, trans. J. Owen, (3 vols., Edinburgh, 1847–51)
John Knox, *Works*	*The Works of John Knox*, ed. D. Laing (4 vols., Edinburgh, 1846–64)
John I	J. Calvin, *Commentaries on the Gospel According to St John 1–10*, trans. T.H.L. Parker, ed. D.W. Torrance and T.F. Torrance (Edinburgh, 1959)
John II	J. Calvin, *Commentary on the Gospel according to John*, trans. W. Pringle (2 vols., Edinburgh, 1847)
I *Peter*	J. Calvin, *Commentaries on the Catholic Epistles*, trans. J. Owen (Edinburgh, 1855)
Psalms	J. Calvin, *Commentary on The Book of Psalms*, trans. J. Anderson (4 vols., Edinburgh, 1845–7)
Registres	*Registres de la Compagnie des pasteurs de Genève au temps de Calvin*, ed. J.F. Bergier and R.M. Kingdon (2 vols., Geneva, 1962–4)
Tracts	J. Calvin *Tracts relating to the Reformation*, trans. H. Beveridge, (4 vols., Edinburgh, 1844–51)

Substantial amounts of Calvin's work have been available in translation for many years, and a great deal of effort was put into publishing edited translations in the middle of the last century by the Calvin Translation Society. These translations have been consulted but, in many instances, substantially modified in the light of the original text and modern English style. In the case of the *Institutes*, the latest translation by F.L. Battles has been used although, again, there have been some modifications in the light of the original Latin and French texts. For this reason, the references give the book (I–IV), chapters (i–) and paragraphs (1–) so that passages can be readily identified in any edition. No attempt has been made to indicate regularly the date of the passages chosen from the *Institutes*. In other translations, the conventional dots indicate omissions but some minor repetitions are passed over without indication.

Acknowledgements

The editors and publishers gratefully acknowledge permission granted by the following to reprint, often with minor modifications, passages from copyright works: SCM Press and the Westminster Press, Philadelphia, for extracts from *The Institutes of the Christian Religion*, trans. F.L. Battles, ed. J.T. McNeill (2 vols., *Library of the Christian Classics*, 1961); E.J. Brill & Co., Leiden, for extracts from Calvin's *Commentary on Seneca's De Clementia*, ed. F.L. Battles and A.M. Hugo (1969).

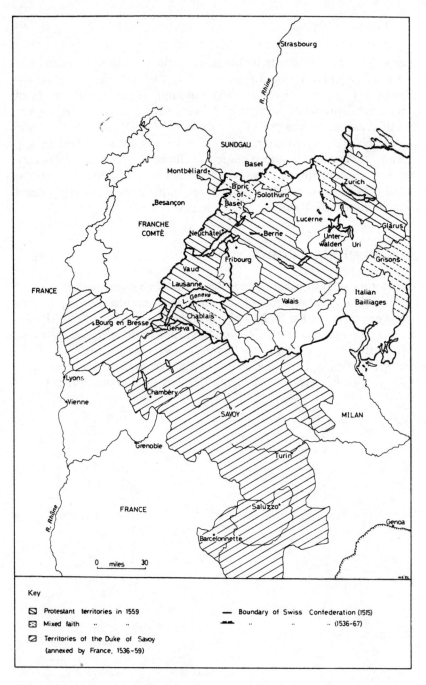

Geneva and its Neighbours in the Time of Calvin

Key

◩ Protestant territories in 1559   —— Boundary of Swiss Confederation (1515)
◪ Mixed faith   „   „   ▬▬ „   „   „   „   (1536–67)
◨ Territories of the Duke of Savoy
   (annexed by France, 1536–59)

Preface

Calvin, it has been said, wrote more during his life than can be read and absorbed during the lifetime of another. Fifty-seven densely-packed volumes of writings were edited and published in the *Corpus Reformatorum*; further sermons have since been published or await an editor. Calvin's enormous correspondence with reformers throughout northern Europe provides a vast source of information about himself, about Geneva, and also about what has been called the 'second-generation' of reform in sixteenth-century Europe.

It is hardly surprising, then, that even this modest book needed two editors. Professor Potter had worked on the manuscript for some time before his death in 1981; what he left was something rather less than half-written and already several times the size of this book. Had he lived, his vast experience as an historian of the Reformation would undoubtedly have enabled him to shape a volume which would have been a fitting sequel to his earlier publication in this series on *Huldrych Zwingli*. Using what he left in the way of notebooks and plans, I have completed something which will undoubtedly reflect my own prejudices and predilections but also, I hope, preserve as much of the quality of Professor Potter's contribution as possible.

This volume complements others in the *Documents of Modern History* series on Martin Luther, Erasmus, Zwingli, and the Reformation in England. For this reason, footnotes to these other works have been introduced to indicate points of comparison and further detail. The illustration on the front cover has been chosen with some care from the numerous (and sometimes unflattering) contemporary sketches, drawings, and paintings of Calvin. It is a portrait of the reformer, painted whilst he was still a young man, perhaps in his early to mid thirties and, therefore, possibly shortly after his return to Geneva in 1541. The artist is unknown but the picture became the property of Theodore Beza, Calvin's successor as head of the Genevan company of pastors. It is slightly idealized but manages to capture a measure of the xvi

earnest, serious, determined, bright-eyed man, still with something of
the lawyer-scholar about him, that I hope will emerge from these
pages.

There are many debts of gratitude, but most especially to Professor
Potter's widow, Mrs R. Potter. She typed and carefully proof-read the
whole manuscript at several stages. She generously allowed me to work
through her husband's papers and notebooks with perfect freedom and
showed great understanding of the difficulties of writing in the midst of
busy university terms. Julia Dagg and the staff of the Sheffield
University Inter-Library Loans department have assisted enormously
in obtaining books quickly and efficiently. Professor James Atkinson
kindly lent the editors his copies of the Calvin Translation Society's
edition of Calvin's works and commented on the finished text.

MG
April 1982

I Early Career

John Calvin (Jean Cauvin) was the most self-effacing of the religious leaders of the Reformation. For many background details in his career, historians have to rely upon the *Life of Calvin* by his fellow exile, compatriot, academic and intimate friend Theodore Beza. Its first draft was hastily completed within three months of Calvin's death in 1564 to accompany the posthumous publication of his commentaries upon the Book of Joshua. This was revised in the following year by another of Calvin's close friends in Geneva, Nicolas Colladon. Ten years later, Beza found the leisure to reorganize the work and it is from this final version that the following extracts are taken. Whilst it was evidently written with the benefit of hindsight, it was clearly based upon personal recollections and appears largely accurate.

During the French civil wars later in the sixteenth century, Roman Catholic apologists attempted to discredit Calvin. Early in the following century, the Dean of the cathedral in Noyon (Calvin's home town and an old ecclesiastical city 60 miles north-east of Paris) undertook an enquiry amongst the local records to substantiate these accusations, and published what he found. He found a great deal of evidence surrounding Calvin's father, Gérard, who was an ecclesiastical official for the cathedral chapter and was eventually excommunicated for careless accounting of ecclesiastical property in November 1528. But there was little to incriminate John Calvin. As Beza's account said, he clearly was intended for the Church at an early age and was appointed a chaplain of an altar in the cathedral at the age of 12. He was permitted to leave the city during the outbreak of plague in August 1523 and this has sometimes been interpreted as indicating the date at which Calvin left Noyon to study in Paris. In fact, he had probably begun his studies there earlier, although he may have returned home during vacations. He was evidently in Paris in 1526, for he failed to attend a chapter meeting and was censured for not providing the required note of absence from the rector of the university. But this did not prevent

Calvin from acquiring a benefice in the following year in the diocese, and he subsequently exchanged this for one at Pont l'Evêque in 1529, the commercial suburb of Noyon, close to the river Oise. Calvin enjoyed the protection of the local bishop, a member of the Montmor family which was the prominent local nobility with strong court connections. He accompanied the bishop's cousins when they went to Paris to study, and he later acknowledged their assistance in the preface to his first major printed work. In another preface, Calvin later paid generous tribute to the importance of his Latin tutor at the college of La Marche in Paris, Mathurin Cordier. Cordier, whose Latin primer remained in use in some French schools until the end of the eighteenth century, was to give him his proficiency in the theologians' language of the day.

A Noyon and Paris

1 Beza's *Life of Calvin*

John Calvin was born at Noyon, a celebrated town in Picardy, or on the borders of Picardy, on 27 July in the year of our Lord 1509. His father's name was Gérard Calvin, his mother's Joan France, both parents being persons of good repute and of adequate means. Gérard was shrewd, prudent and highly thought of by most of the nobility of the region, and this was why the young Calvin was from his boyhood very well educated, though at his father's expense, in the family of the Montmor, one of the most distinguished in that region. Having afterwards accompanied them to Paris in the continuance of his studies, his tutor in the college of La Marche was Mathurin Cordier, a man of great worth and erudition and in the highest repute in almost all the schools in France as a teacher of the young. He attained the age of 85, and died (the same year as Calvin) at Geneva, whilst a professor in the Academy in that city. Calvin afterwards went to the college of Montaigu, and there had for his tutor a Spaniard, and a man of considerable attainments. Under him, Calvin, who was most diligent, made such progress that he left his fellow students behind in the course on grammar and was promoted to the study of Dialectics and what is called Arts.

His father had at first intended him for the study of Theology, to which he inferred that Calvin had a natural inclination; for even at that tender age he was remarkably religious and was also a strict censor of everything vicious in his companions. This I remember having heard it from some Catholics, impeccable witnesses, many years after he became famous. Being thus destined as it were to sacred office, his father procured for him a benefice from the bishop of Noyon, in what is called the cathedral church, and thereafter the benefice of a parish connected to a suburban village called Pont l'Evêque, the birth-place of his father, who had lived there until he had moved into the town. It is certain that Calvin preached several sermons (though not in priest's orders) in this place before he left France.

Tracts I, pp. lix–lx (*CR* XLIX, col. 121)

2 Appointment as chaplain (1521)

19 May 1521. M. Jacques Regnard, secretary to the Reverend Father in God Charles de Hangest, bishop of Noyon, reported to the chapter that the vicars-general of the said bishop have given to John, aged 12, son of Gérard Calvin, a portion of the chapel of La Gésine.

A. Lefranc, *La Jeunesse de Calvin* (Paris, 1888), p. 195

3 A dedication (1532)

I owe you [the Montmor family] all that I am and have. . . . As a boy I was brought up in your home and was initiated in my studies with you. Hence I owe to your noble family my first training in life and letters.

Battles and Hugo, pp. 12–13

4 A dedication to Mathurin Cordier (1550)

When I was a child and had merely grasped the rudiments of Latin, my father sent me to Paris. There, through the goodness of God, you were my tutor for a while and taught me the true way to learn so that I could continue with greater profit. When you were in charge of the top class you were very successful. But you realized that other masters were being too ambitious and teaching boys to show off knowledge for which they lacked a solid grasp. Growing tired of this, you went to teach in the lowest class for a year. This was clearly your purpose and, for me, it was a fortunate beginning to the study of Latin which occurred by the special blessing of God. I enjoyed your teaching only for a short while since we were then moved up a class by that stupid man who directed our studies according to his own notions, or rather, his personal whim. Yet I was so assisted by you that, whatever progress I have made since then, I gladly ascribe to you.

CR XLI, cols. 525–6

B The Humanist

Humanism was the great solvent of traditional ways of thinking and accepted notions in the sixteenth century. For Calvin it meant a new direction to his career and a further degree course at the university of Orléans. It also involved the acquisition of another language, Greek. Calvin learnt the latest techniques of textual philology and how to apply them. Finally he acquired an abiding interest in the nature of law, justice and equity which stayed with him for the rest of his life.

The reasons that Calvin and his father both decided that his future lay in the law are not entirely clear but, having obtained a degree of Master of Arts from Paris, perhaps in the course of the academic year 1525–6, Calvin moved to Orléans because Paris university had no law faculty. The traditional texts of the law degree were the law codes, digests and institutes of Justinian, the *Corpus iuris civilis*. Under the impact of the Renaissance, commentaries and lectures were being undertaken on the original texts rather than upon the medieval glosses upon the texts. Amongst the pioneers of this technique in France was Andrea Alciato, a famous Italian jurist. Calvin, as well as other students from Orléans, went to hear Alciato give his inaugural lectures in the newly constructed law school at Bourges in 1529–30. Calvin subsequently became licensed to take his doctorate in law in 1530–1 and he also undertook some lecturing at the university in Orléans.

Calvin made many friends whilst he studied law. They included the able, liberal and tolerant Pierre Robert, called Olivetanus ('Midnight Oil') because, like Calvin, he worked so much at night. Olivetanus left Orléans hurriedly in 1528 and retired to Strasbourg under fear of persecution; this may be the first indication of Calvin's involvement with heterodoxy. To a German professor from Rottweil called

Melchior Wolmar, Calvin owed his initiation to Greek as well as his ability to handle his critics with patience.

In June 1531, Calvin went to Paris, probably to follow the lectures of the new professors appointed by the king, Francis I, which were taking place there. He also finished his first book, which was a humanist commentary upon a famous classical text, that on *Clemency* by Seneca (*De Clementia*). It subsequently appeared in 1532. Calvin based his work on the text already prepared and published by Erasmus in 1529, but he applied to the commentary all the resources of his newly acquired legal and classical learning, a wide knowledge of Roman history, his powers of textual analysis and criticism, and an analysis of Stoic philosophy. Even if Calvin did not entirely concur with the Stoic sentiments of Seneca, they undoubtedly influenced his theology later on.

5 Studying law at Orléans

The idea of making Calvin a priest was interrupted by a change in the views of both father and son – in the former because he saw that the law was a surer road to wealth and fame and in the latter because, having been acquainted with the reformed faith through a relative named Pierre Robert Olivétan (the person to whom the churches of France owe that translation of the Old Testament from the Hebrew which was printed at Neuchâtel[1]), he had begun to devote himself to the study of the holy scriptures, and from an abhorrence of all kinds of superstition, to discontinue his attendance at the public services of the church.

Having set out for Orléans to study law, which was taught there by Pierre de l'Estoile, the most distinguished French lawyer of that period, Calvin made such astonishing progress in a short while that he often deputized for the professor and was considered rather a teacher than a pupil. Upon his departure, he was presented with a Doctor's degree, free of expense and with the unanimous consent of all the professors, as a return for the services which he had rendered the Academy. Meanwhile, however, he diligently cultivated the study of sacred literature and made such progress that all in the city who desired to become acquainted with a purer religion often called to consult him and were impressed with his learning and enthusiasm. Some of them who are still alive and who were on close terms with him then say that

---

[1] Published in 1534 with a preface by Calvin.

his custom at that time was, after dining very frugally, to continue studying until midnight and, upon waking in the morning, to spend some time in meditation and, as it were, to digest what he had read in bed; they say that, whilst he was thus involved, he was very unwilling to be disturbed. By these prodigious vigils, he undoubtedly acquired a solid learning and an excellent memory; but it is probable that he also contracted a weakness of the stomach which afterwards brought on various diseases and ultimately led to his untimely death.

The Academy at Bourges had, at that time, acquired great fame through Andrea Alciato (undoubtedly the greatest lawyer of the age) who had been invited there from Italy. Calvin thought it right to go and study under him too. He accordingly went there and, on grounds both literary and religious, formed a friendship with Melchior Wolmar, a German from Rottweil and a professor of Greek. I have the greatest pleasure in mentioning his name because he was my own teacher and the only one I had from boyhood through to my youth. His learning, piety and other virtues, together with his admirable qualities as a teacher cannot be adequately praised. On his suggestion and with his assistance, Calvin learned Greek. The recollection of this benefit which he thus received from Wolmar he later publicly acknowledged by dedicating to him his *Commentary upon the First Epistle to the Corinthians*. . . . A sudden intimation of the death of his father called him back to his native town. Shortly afterwards, aged 24, he went to Paris and there wrote his excellent commentary upon Seneca's treatise *De Clementia*. This very grave writer was obviously in tune with Calvin's disposition and was a great favourite with him.

Tracts I, pp. lx—lxii (*CR* IL, cols. 121-2)

6   Commentary upon the *De Clementia* of Seneca (1532)

Seneca, in his first chapter, caused the emperor Nero to reflect upon the sovereignty of the laws, even over rulers.

Seneca's Text: Sternness I keep hidden, but clemency ever ready to hand. I so hold guard over myself as though I were about to render an account to those laws which I have summoned from neglect and darkness into day.

Calvin's Comment: He has well added 'as though' because the prince has been released from obedience to the laws; but it is a saying worthy of a ruler's majesty for a prince to confess himself 'bound to the laws'.

'And surely there is something greater than rule in submitting the prince to the laws' it says [*Codex Just.* 1.xiv.4].

In the following chapter, Seneca dispels the view that clemency upholds the wicked at the expense of the virtuous whilst admitting that certain people are so evil that clemency is inappropriate to them.

Seneca's Text: Besides, there are a great many people who might be turned back [by the exercise of clemency] towards good behaviour.[1] Nevertheless, it is not fitting to pardon too commonly; for when the distinction between good and bad men is removed, the result is confusion and an epidemic of vice.[2] Therefore a moderation should be exercised which will be capable of distinguishing between curable and incurable characters.[3]

Calvin's Comment: 1. . . . This is exactly what clemency does. It is of great importance when pleading for mercy, says Quintillian (7.iv.18) 'if there is hope that a man will live innocently in the future and make himself of use to others'. Or, as Cicero says, 'repentance is the best haven after a shipwreck'. . . .

2. The sages define virtue as the mean which lies, to quote Cicero, . . .' between too much and too little' and one must guard clemency, lapsed into excess, from being ascribed to vice rather than to virtue. One must grant pardon, but not to all men. For some persons are improved by pardon, others are corrupted. . . .

3. Now he marks the reason why pardon should not be commonly given; there are many persons so depraved and profligate that, unless they are constrained by punishment, they will immediately break down every restraint of shame and decency. Here let the judge remember 'By tolerating an old injustice, a new one is provoked'. Let him set before himself Cicero's statement . . . 'There is no temptation to crime so powerful as the prospect of impunity'. . . .

Battles and Hugo, pp. 21, 43, 65–73

C Conversion and Exile

Calvin was a 'second-generation' reformer. By the time he went to study in Paris, Lutheranism was already a problem for the authorities. The Sorbonne condemned Luther's works in 1521 upon the active encouragement of Noel Bédier, principal of the college of Montaigu, where Calvin spent part of his time of study. The *parlement* of Paris, the influential sovereign law court sitting in the capital, became the Sorbonne's ally and rapidly banned all available translations of scripture into the vernacular, whether Lutheran or Erasmian. These early moves by the authorities gave to French 'evangelism' (an appropriate historical term describing the various coteries of printers, preachers, scholars and students who were especially concerned to read the scriptures in the vernacular, but were not necessarily Lutherans) its characteristic features. The *parlement*'s edicts were moderated by the king, Francis I, upon pressure from Lutheran princes abroad and his own sister, Marguerite of Navarre, a remarkable lady who protected the 'evangelists' as far as possible. But when the king and court were away from Paris, as in 1525–7, the *parlement* was able to be more repressive.

From Beza's account, Calvin appears to mature directly and without hesitation within the evangelical environment. However, Calvin provides two autobiographical reflections which make it clear that he had no dramatic revelation or deep spiritual moment of conversion and that his progress towards the reform was irregular and oblique. There was an initial kindling of enthusiasm at some unspecified date, but possibly after he had taken his Master's degree in Paris. There then followed a period when Calvin's timidity and shyness (or, perhaps, his stubbornness and a certain respect for the established church) made him either uncommitted, or, if committed, highly discreet.

Active repression of the reform movement was eventually responsible for bringing Calvin into the open. It began in October 1533 and was to lead to his exile from Paris and then, in the following year, from France. Towards the end of the 1520s, the authorities were increasingly alarmed at the appearance in France of what was loosely known as Zwinglianism. In its French context, Zwinglianism was believed to be 'iconoclastic' (the first outbreak of image-smashing in Paris was in June 1528) and 'sacramentarian', encouraging attacks on the mass and the Catholic dogma of the Real Presence. In October 1533 the king was in the south of France and the Sorbonne and the *parlement* seized the initiative. The following month the university's rector, Nicolas Cop, preached his rectorial address taking the Beatitudes as his text. It was a sermon with Erasmian and Lutheran quotations in it and strong evangelist undercurrents. Beza says that Calvin actually wrote it (but that now seems unlikely, although he did possess a copy of it) and, following the sermon, Calvin's rooms in Paris were searched and his letters were confiscated. In haste, Calvin followed Cop and fled from the capital to stay with one of his friends, Louis du Tillet in Angoulême. Du Tillet sheltered him and allowed him to use his father's substantial library. From there, Calvin went to Nérac to the court of Marguerite of Navarre and met Lefèvre d'Etaples. In 1534 events moved more rapidly. In May Calvin resigned all his benefices in Noyon. He moved quickly from place to place in the country, perhaps to avoid suspicion, and only once visited Paris, apparently to meet the Spanish exile, Michael Servetus (*see below*, part V). This fugitive existence was abruptly terminated in October 1534 by the famous affair of the *Placards*. These were broadsheets printed at Neuchâtel where two preachers of Zwinglian persuasion, Guillaume Farel and Antoine Marcourt were very active. Copies of the posters were distributed widely in Paris and as far away as Amboise where the king was staying. With the news of the Anabaptist uprising taking place at Münster in everyone's mind, and the fears of sacramentalism running high, the *parlement* of Paris, with the king's subsequent approval, set about enforcing harsher measures against the printing and distribution of suspect literature, the harbouring of suspect heretics and legal delays to their prompt trial and despatch. Calvin's friend and the owner of the house where he often stayed in Paris, Etienne de La Forge, was arrested and subsequently burned in February 1535. Calvin decided to leave the country but his escape was nearly abandoned when one of the servants ran off with the money and one of the horses. He eventually arrived in January 1535 in Basel, the Imperial Free City and eye of the Protestant storm elsewhere in Europe. The elderly Erasmus, Heinrich Bullinger (Zwingli's friend and successor at Zurich), Guillaume Farel, Pierre Robert Olivetanus, Nicolas Cop were already there; and Calvin set to work to complete his *Institutes of the Christian Religion*.

7 Calvin – unwilling convert

The more closely I examined myself, the sharper became the stings of conscience which pricked me, so much so that my only relief lay in deceiving myself and forgetting about it. Since nothing better offered itself, I continued upon the career I had begun. Then, however, there arose another form of doctrine which was not to turn away from the profession of Christianity but to take it back to its own source and to restore it, cleansed of all its corruptions, to its essential purity. Offended by this novel notion, at first I listened reluctantly to it and, I must confess, resisted it with strength and vigour. It is natural to be stubborn and obstinate and continue in a predetermined course of action and I was only persuaded with the greatest difficulty to confess that I had been in ignorance and error all my life. One thing, especially, prevented me from believing these new teachers, and that was reverence for the Church. But after I listened to them attentively for some time and allowed myself to be instructed by them, I perceived that my fear that it would weaken the majesty of the Church was groundless. For they explained how great a difference there is between schism from the Church and the study of ways to correct the corruptions which contaminated it.

> From *Calvin's Reply to the letter by Cardinal Sadoleto to the Senate and People of Geneva*, 1539 (*CR* XXXIII, col. 412)

8 Calvin – discreet convert

So it came to pass that I was withdrawn from the study of arts and was transferred to the study of law. I endeavoured faithfully to apply myself to this, in obedience to my father's wishes. But God, by the secret hand of his providence, eventually pointed my life in a different direction.

At first, I was so obstinately devoted to the superstitions of the Papacy (and more stubbornly so than was right for someone of my age) that I was not easily extricated from so profound an abyss. Then God, by a sudden conversion, changed and shaped my heart towards being more receptive. Having received some taste and inkling of the true piety, I was immediately stirred up to enthusiasm for it and, although I did not immediately put to one side all my other studies, I pursued them more spasmodically. But I was amazed to discover that, within a year, all those around with a similar yearning for the pure doctrine, came to me for assistance, even though I was only a novice myself. For my part, being rather shy and preferring tranquillity and repose, I began to look for some quiet retreat from them. But, no sooner had I found what I wanted than, on the contrary, these places of retreat turned into public schools. Despite my wish always to live in obscurity and retirement, God so moved and transformed me through a variety of experiences and never left me in peace anywhere until, contrary to my natural inclinations, he brought me towards enlightenment and, so to speak, forced me into the open.

> Calvin's Introduction to the *Commentary upon the book of Psalms*, 1557 (*CR* LVIX, cols. 22–4)

9   Calvin and Nicolas Cop

About this time, Calvin renouncing all other studies, devoted himself to God, to the great delight of all the pious ones who were then meeting secretly in Paris. It was not long before an event required all their efforts.

At this time Nicolas Cop, son of Guillaume Cop of Basel, physician to the king, had been appointed rector in the university of Paris. According to the custom, he had to deliver an oration on 1 November, the feast of All Saints' Day to the papists, and Calvin provided him with a sermon in which religion was dealt with more trenchantly and with greater purity than had generally been the case in the past. This was intolerable to the Sorbonne and also disapproved of by the Senate or *Parlement*, which called the rector to appear before it. He accordingly set out with his officers but, being warned on the way to take heed of his enemies, he turned back home and afterwards left the country and retired to Basel. Searches were made at the college of Fortret where Calvin happened to be residing. He was not at home but his papers were seized and, amongst them, numerous letters from his friends. Worst of all, this gravely endangered the lives of many of them, for these judges were very harsh against the Church, especially one of them called Jean Morin, whose savage proceedings are well-remembered. This tempest the Lord dispersed by means of the queen of Navarre, only sister to King Francis, a woman of admirable intelligence and, at this time, a patroness of the Reformers. Inviting Calvin to her court, she received him and listened to him with the greatest respect.

> *Tracts* I, pp. lxii–lxiii (*CR* XLIX, col. 124)

10   Nicolas Cop's oration, 1 November 1533

'Blessed are the poor in spirit' (Matthew 5). . . . In the beginning, it is to be carefully considered what the point of this scripture is, for by that

we can explain it; and we will more easily understand it when we have
defined and compared what we mean by the law and the gospel. Now
the gospel is good news and the saving grace preached by Christ who
was sent from God the Father to be the hope for all of us that he will
grant us everlasting life. Law is contained in precepts, it controls, it
constrains, it can promise no benevolence. The gospel does all these
things but, instead of compelling people by precepts, it leads them
towards the full benevolence of God. Whoever wants this passage of
scripture purely and simply expounded will examine everything in the
light of these definitions. Those who cannot follow this line of reasoning will never be happy with the philosophy of Christ . . .

CR XXXVIII, col. 31

11   The Placards

The year 1534 became notorious for the savage treatment of many of
the Reformers. Gérard Roussel, a doctor of the Sorbonne, but much
enamoured of the new doctrines, and also Corald, of the order of St
Augustine who, aided by the queen of Navarre, had done much during
this and the previous year to promote the cause of Christ in Paris, were
not only driven from the pulpit but thrown into prison. The rage of the
cursed monarch Francis I was aroused to such a pitch by certain
broadsheets against the mass, which had been circulated in the city and
even fixed to the door of the king's own bed-chamber, that the king
attended a public fast. He went to the church accompanied by his three
children with his head bare and carrying a blazing torch as a kind of
expiation, and then ordered 32 martyrs to be burned alive (eight of
each in the four most public places in the city). . . . Calvin published
his remarkable treatise entitled *Psychopannychia* against the error of
those who, reviving a doctrine which had been held in former times,
taught that the soul, when separated from the body falls asleep.[2]
Shortly afterwards, perceiving the state of affairs there, he decided to
leave France. Accordingly, in the company of the man with whom he
had lodged for some time in Saintonge, he set out to Basel by way of
Lorraine.

Tracts I, pp. lxiv–lxv (CR XLIX, col. 124)

[2] Calvin's treatise on the notion of the sleep of the soul does not, in fact, appear to have
been published until 1542. Luther and Zwingli had already written extensively on the
subject and the Anabaptists, the 'nefarious herd' and 'perversity of this age' as Calvin
called them, speculated a great deal on it too. For this reason, given the rising at
Münster, if Calvin's treatise had been written at the date which Beza suggests, it was at
an appropriate moment. Calvin later disallowed prayers for the repose of the souls of the
departed but accepted that the souls of the elect were, in some way, actively associated
with the praise of God after the death of the body.

II   *The Institutes of the Christian Religion*

A The Making of the *Institutes*

Calvin's most sustained contribution to theology lies in his *Institutes of the Christian Religion* (*Christianae Religionis Institutio*). By the time of his death, it had become the Protestant theologian's equivalent to the lawyer's institutes of Justinian. But when it was first published in the Latin edition by the famous Basel printers, Thomas Platter and Balthasar Lasius in March 1536, the *Institutes* was intended to be a short textbook of reformed orthodoxy whose clarity of exposition would make it as useful as Melanchthon's *Common Places* (*Loci Communes*, 1521) or William Farel's *Summary or Brief Declaration of Matters very necessary for a Christian* (*Sommaire . . .*, 1534). For this reason, the form of the book was based upon the framework of the catechism with six chapters on the Law, Faith, Prayer, the Sacraments, Grace and Liberty. But it was also intended as an apology for the French evangelicals against the repression undertaken with royal support after the affair of the Placards. For this reason, there was a long introductory preface addressed to Francis I. It was a sustained defence of the evangelicals against the unjust persecution inflicted upon them and an argument for their being the legitimate heirs of the early Christian Church and, unlike the Anabaptists, unpossessed of any seditious intentions.

The first edition was a considerable success and sold out within a year of publication. Successive editions transformed it, whilst still preserving the essential theological components upon which it was based. It eventually became a systematic theology based upon the Bible, a manual to ethics, a guidebook to the Protestant creed and a comprehensive survey to Reformation theological controversy. In July 1539 a new Latin edition was printed in Strasbourg in which a preface to the reader was added. This suggested for the first time that Calvin was aiming to provide a theological 'summa', equivalent to the works of theology produced by the medieval scholastics like St Thomas Aquinas. With the addition of many new chapters, the book became three times its original length. Much of the expansion consisted of the exposition of scriptural passages sustaining his theology, and Calvin at this point began to conceive of the work as a doctrinal compendium to a series of commentaries upon individual books of the Bible and therefore of particular value to both the theology student and the interested lay reader.

The expansions of the text undertaken in 1539 and again in 1543 and 1550 also revealed the growing weight of Calvin's learning in the Church fathers and the scholastics. Many of his additions were designed to answer the criticisms of his doctrinal formulations raised in Geneva and elsewhere in print in Europe. For this reason, the final Latin edition of the *Institutes* in 1559 had to be completely recast in order to preserve a formal, logical basis to the work. Calvin arranged it around the basic progression of the Apostles' Creed with the chapters distributed into four books: 'On the Knowledge of God the Creator'; 'The Knowledge of God the Redeemer'; 'The Way in Which we Receive the Grace of Christ'; and finally, 'The External Means or Aids by Which God Invites us into the Society of Christ'. Within these books, the chapters are clearly subdivided and cross-referenced to create a theology with a great sense of its own internal unity. Calvin translated the early edition into French in 1541 and dictated another French translation of the final edition in 1560. It has subsequently been translated into several languages, into English no less than four times, not counting abridgements and adaptations. The first English translation was in 1561 by Thomas Norton and the most recent one in 1961 by F.L. Battles.

12   Preface addressed to Francis I, King of France (Basel, 23 August 1535)

When I first set my hand to this work, nothing was further from my mind, most glorious King, than to write something that might after-wards be offered to Your Majesty. My purpose was solely to transmit certain rudiments by which those who are touched with any zeal for religion might be shaped to true godliness. I undertook this task especially with our French countrymen in mind, many of whom I knew to be craving for Christ although I found very few of them had been

properly imbued with even a slight knowledge of him. The book itself is
a proof that this was my intention, adapted as it is to a simple and, you
may say, elementary form of teaching.

But I perceived that the violence of certain wicked persons has
dominated your realm so far that there is no place in it for sound
doctrine. Consequently it seemed to me that I should be doing some
good if I gave instruction to them and made a confession before you in
the same work. From this you may learn about the nature of the
doctrine against which those madmen burn with rage who today
disturb your realm with fire and sword. I am not afraid, in fact, to
confess that here is contained almost the sum of that doctrine which
they proclaim must be punished by imprisonment, exile, proscription,
burning and extermination by land and sea. I know that terrible
reports have reached your eyes and mind, designed to render our cause
as hateful as possible to you. But, as befits your clemecy, you ought to
weigh the fact that if it is sufficient merely to rely upon an accusation,
then no innocence will remain in either words or deeds. . . .

For this reason, most invincible King, I ask you in justice to undertake a full enquiry into the case which until now has been handled
– one might say tossed around – without due process of law and with
heated fury rather than judicious gravity. Do not think that I am here
preparing my own personal defence, so that I can return to my native
land. Even though I regard my country with as much natural affection
as becomes me, as things now stand I do not much regret being
excluded from it. Rather, I embrace the common cause of all believers,
that of Christ himself – a cause completely torn and trampled upon in
your realm at this moment, lying, as it were, utterly neglected, more as
a result of the tyranny of certain Pharisees than as a result of your
approval. . . .

They do not cease to assail our doctrine and to reproach and defame
it with names that render it hated and suspected. They call it 'new' and
of a 'recent birth'. They reproach it as 'doubtful and uncertain'. They
ask what miracles have given it confirmation. They enquire whether it
is right for it to prevail against the accepted opinions of so many holy
fathers and against most ancient custom. They urge us to acknowledge
that it is schismatic because it wages war against the Church or that the
Church was lifeless during the many centuries when no such thing was
heard of. Finally, they say that there is no need for many arguments for
one can judge by its fruits what it is, seeing that it has given birth to
such a heap of sects, so many seditious tumults, such great licentious-

ness. Indeed it is very easy for them to revile a foresaken cause before the credulous and ignorant multitude. But if we too might speak in our turn, this bitterness which they licentiously and with impunity spew at us from their swollen cheeks would subside. . . .

And we are unjustly charged, too, with intentions of a kind which we have never in the least encouraged, namely that we contrive the over-throw of kingdoms. We, from whom not one seditious word was ever heard; we, whose life was always acknowledged to be quiet and simple when we lived under your authority; we, who do not cease to pray for the full prosperity of yourself and your kingdom although we are now exiles from our own homes! We are, apparently, chasing wildly after every vice! Even if in our way of life many things are blameworthy, there is nothing that deserves such serious reproach. And we have not, by God's grace, profited so little by the gospel that our life may not be for these objectors an example of chastity, generosity, mercy, temperance, patience, modesty, and all other virtues. It is perfectly clear that we fear and worship God in truth since we seek in life and death alike that his name be hallowed. And hatred itself has been forced to bear witness to the innocence and civic uprightness of some of us upon whom the punishment of death was inflicted for that one thing which ought to have received special praise.

Institutes, pp. 9–10, 11, 30

13   Preface addressed to the reader (1 August 1559)

In the first edition of this work of ours, I did not in the least expect that success which, of his infinite goodness, the Lord has given it. Thus, for the most part, I treated the subject summarily, as is usually the case in small books. But when I realized that it was received by almost all godly men with an acclaim which I would never have ventured to hope for, much less to imagine, I deeply felt that I was much more favoured than I had deserved to be. Consequently I thought that I would be extremely ungracious not to try, at least to the best of my slender ability, to respond to this warm appreciation for me, an appreciation which demanded my further diligence. Not only did I attempt this in the second edition, but each time the work has been reprinted since then, it has been enriched with some additions. Although I do not regret the labour spent on it, I was never satisfied until the work was arranged in the order now set forth. I trust now that I have provided something that will win universal approval. . . .

I can furnish a clear testimony of my great zeal and effort to carry out this task for God's Church. Last winter, when I thought the quartan fever was about to lead to my death, the more the disease pressed upon me, the less I spared myself, until I could leave a book behind me that might, in some measure, repay the generous invitation of godly men. Indeed I should have preferred to have done it sooner, but it is done soon enough if it is done well enough. God has filled me with zeal to spread his kingdom and to further the public good. I am also equally clear in my own conscience and I have God and the angels to be my witness that, since I undertook the office of teacher in the Church, I have had no other purpose than to benefit the Church by the maintenance of the pure doctrine of godliness. But I think that there is no one who has been assailed, bitten and wounded by more false accusations than I have been. . . .

Moreover it has been my purpose in this labour to prepare and instruct candidates in sacred theology for the reading of the divine Word in order that they may be able both to have easy access to it and to advance without stumbling. For I believe that I have so embraced the sum of religion in all its parts, and have arranged it in such an order, that if anyone rightly grasps it, it will not be difficult for him to determine what he ought especially to seek in scripture and to what end he ought to relate its contents. If, after this road has, as it were, been paved, I shall publish any interpretations of scripture; I shall always condense them, because I shall have no need to undertake long doctrinal discussions and to digress into commonplaces. In this way the godly reader will be spared great annoyance and boredom, provided that he approach scripture armed with a knowledge of the present work as a necessary tool.

Institutes, pp. 3–5

B Knowledge of God and of Ourselves

The opening sentence of the *Institutes* presents this as its theme. Eternal, the creator of the universe and of men, perfect in wisdom and goodness, omnipotent, a spirit transcendant everywhere, Calvin's God is in heaven but also everywhere else at the same time. He is revealed to man in the Bible, and references to the scriptures are constant. With their assistance, Calvin establishes an orthodox picture of God against what he regarded as the fruitless and unorthodox speculations of the Renaissance followers of Epicurus, Democritus, Lucretius and the neo-Platonists. His own approach, when writing of God, was especially to emphasize him as a sovereign ruler, a righteous and merciful judge. Contemporary French legal thinking upon sovereignty and upon the perfect judge can hardly have escaped Calvin whilst he had been at Orléans. Inevitably there was an undercurrent of criticism of the Roman Catholic Church, and especially of its idolatry, as Calvin conceived it. But Calvin accepted, along with Roman Catholic theologians, the orthodoxy of the Trinity. He admitted that there was no specifically Biblical use of the term but regarded it as a necessary theological conclusion from what the Bible says, and therefore a reality. The passages upon the Trinity were expanded and given a new emphasis in the final edition of the *Institutes* as a result of the disputes that Calvin had conducted with anti-Trinitarians like Servetus.

14

All our wisdom, in so far as it is held to be true and perfect, consists of two things; namely a right knowledge of God and of ourselves.

Institutes I, i, 1

15

Although our mind cannot apprehend God without rendering to him some honour, it will not be sufficient simply to accept that there is One whom all ought to honour and adore unless we are also persuaded that he is the fountain of all goodness and that we must seek nothing elsewhere but in him. This I take to mean that, not only does he sustain this universe (as he once founded it) by his boundless might, regulate it by his wisdom, preserve it by his goodness, and especially rule mankind by his righteousness and judgement, bear with it in his mercy, watch over it by his protection, but also that no drop will be found of wisdom, light, righteousness, power, rectitude or genuine truth which does not flow from him and of which he is not the cause. Thus we may learn to await and seek all these things from him and thankfully ascribe them, once revealed, to him. This sense of the powers of God teaches us the full meaning of piety from which religion is born. I call 'piety' that reverence joined with a love of God which the knowledge of his benefits induces.

Institutes I, ii, 1

16

The pious mind also deems it right and meet to observe God's authority in all things, reverence his majesty, take care to advance his glory and obey his commandments. He is envisaged by the pious mind as a righteous judge, armed with severity to punish wickedness, whose judgement seat is ever before its gaze so that the fear of provoking his anger is a constant restraint. And yet it is not so terrified by the awareness of his judgement as to wish to run away, even if some way of escape were open. It embraces him not only as a punisher of the wicked but also as a benefactor of the pious. For the pious mind realizes that the punishment of the impious and wicked and the reward of life eternal for the righteous equally are part of God's glory. Besides, this mind restrains itself from sinning, not out of fear of punishment alone, but because it loves and reveres God as Father, it worships and adores him as Lord. . . . Here indeed is pure and real religion. Faith so joined with an earnest fear of God.

Institutes I, ii, 2

17–18   Against idolatry

If the papists have any shame, let them henceforward not evade the issue by saying that pictures are the books of the uneducated, because it is plainly refuted by very many testimonies of scripture. Even if I were to grant them this, yet they would not thus gain by much in their defence of their idols. It is well-known that they set monstrosities of this kind in place of God. The pictures or statues that they dedicate to saints – what are they but examples of the most depraved lust and obscenity? If anyone wished to model himself after them, he would be fit for the lash. Indeed, brothels show prostitutes dressed more virtuously and modestly than the churches show those objects which they wish to be thought of as images of virgins.

Institutes I, xi, 7

18

Because sculpture and painting are gifts of God, I seek a pure and legitimate use of each, lest those things which the Lord has conferred upon us for his glory and our good be not only polluted by perverse misuse but also turned to our destruction. . . . It remains that only those things are to be sculptured or painted which the eyes are capable of seeing: let not God's majesty, which is far above the perception of the eyes, be debased through unseemly representations.

Institutes I, xi, 12

19 Trinity

Now although the heretics ridicule the word 'person' and certain squeamish men cry out against admitting a term fashioned by the human mind, they cannot shake our conviction that three are spoken of, each of which is entirely God, yet that there is not more than one God. What wickedness, then, it is to disapprove of words that explain nothing else than what is attested and sealed by scripture! . . . If they call a foreign word one that cannot be shown to stand written, syllable by syllable in scripture, they are indeed imposing upon us an unjust law which condemns all interpretations not patched together out of the fabric of the scriptures. . . . What is to be said, then, when it has been proved that the Church is utterly compelled to make use of the words 'Trinity' and 'Persons'? If anyone should find fault with the novelty of the words, does he not deserve to be judged as bearing the light of truth unworthily, since he is finding fault only with what renders the truth plain and clear?

Institutes I, xiii, 3

C The Word

The scriptures were central to the whole of Calvin's thought. They contained the word of God, dictated to mortals by the Holy Spirit who alone was their true expositor. Like Luther and Zwingli, Calvin assumed that the Bible, properly understood, could not be wrong. Every sentence and phrase was reconcilable with every other, and, by the date of the last edition of the *Institutes*, Calvin had commented upon many of the books of the Bible in print and expounded others in sermons. The world, created 6,000 years ago, was the centre of the universe, Adam was the first man, only eight human beings survived the Flood, every miracle occurred exactly as stated, Jonah was three days in the belly of the great fish and the sun stood still over Gideon. There was no need to go outside the pages of the Bible for the whole of truth was contained within it. Human traditions, however venerable, could be ignored and the visible Church had no meaning except as a result of God's Word.

There was nothing magical about the Bible's words, however, and Calvin was well aware that copyists were fallible and that a knowledge of the original biblical languages would be invaluable for its exposition. He put the techniques that he had learned, and already displayed in the analysis of Seneca's text, into practice with holy scripture. He was not surprised that there were detailed inconsistencies in the Bible and he accepted the possibility that letters from St Paul could have been lost. He never commented upon the Apocalyptic passages of scripture and regarded them with suspicion. In the interpretation of the Bible, Calvin accepted that the Holy Spirit, acting through a man's conscience, had to inform and illuminate every fallible human judgement which had to be made. This illumination did not come automatically or to every one. Anabaptists and others who claimed to have a special inspiration from the Spirit for the interpretation of the scriptures were to be as much mistrusted as the Roman Catholics who reduced scripture to insignificance.

The Word was made law in the Old Testament, and Calvin's lawyer's sensitivities seized upon the Mosaic Law, encapsulated in the Commandments as a basic text which was still binding upon all Christians provided that it corresponded with the teachings of Christ. He also took up the concept of the covenant made by God with Abraham, and thence to the Patriarchs and David and so, through Christ, to all elect Christians, a series of promises between God and his chosen people.

The New Testament provided in God the Son, Christ, the eternal Word, a great mediator who had been foretold in the Old Testament and who would both reveal the essence of God's law and help fallen mankind to obey it. The whole of the second book of the *Institutes* was concerned with God the redeemer in Christ who was crucified by God's eternal will, rose, ascended and was glorified in heaven and who would come again at the day of judgement to reconcile man to God when the elect would be separated from the reprobate. Until then, he alone was head of the Church and present in the Lord's Supper.

20   The Word

By his Word, God rendered faith unambiguous forever, a faith that should be superior to all opinion. Finally, in order that truth might abide forever in the world with a continuing succession of teaching and survive through all ages, the same oracles he had given to the patriarchs it was his pleasure to have recorded, as it were, on public tablets. With this intent the law was published, and the prophets afterwards added as its interpreters. For even though the use of the law was manifold, as will be seen more clearly in its place, it was specially committed to Moses and all the prophets to teach the way of reconciliation between God and men, whence also Paul calls 'Christ the end of the law' (Romans 10, 4). I repeat once more; besides the specific doctrine of faith and repentance that sets forth Christ as mediator, scripture adorns with unmistakable marks and tokens the one true God, in that he has created and governs the universe, in order that he may not be mixed up with the throng of false gods. Therefore, however fitting it may be for man seriously to turn his eyes to contemplate God's works, since he has been placed in this glorious theatre [nature] to be a spectator of them, it is fitting that he listen to the Word, the better to profit. . . . Now, in order that true religion may shine upon us, we ought to hold that it must take its beginning from heavenly doctrine and that no one can get even the slightest taste of right and sound beliefs unless he is a pupil of scripture. Hence there also emerges the beginning of true understanding when we reverently embrace what it pleases God there to witness of himself. But not only faith, perfect and in every way complete, but all right knowledge of God is born of obedience.

Institutes I, vi, 2

21-2   Scripture and the Holy Spirit

Those whom the Holy Spirit has inwardly taught rest truly upon scripture and scripture is indeed self-authenticated. Hence it is wrong to subject it to proof and reasoning. And the certainty it deserves with us, it attains by the testimony of the Spirit. For even if it wins reverence for itself by its own majesty, it seriously affects us only when it is sealed upon our hearts through the Spirit. Therefore, illumined by his power, we believe neither by our own nor by anyone else's judgement that scripture is from God; but above human judgement we affirm with utter certainty (just as if we were gazing upon the majesty of God himself) that it has flowed to us from the very mouth of God by the ministry of men. We seek no proofs, no marks of genuineness upon which our judgement may lean; but we subject our judgement and wit to it as to a thing far beyond any guesswork.

Institutes I, viii, 5

22

By this one word we may refute all the inventions which Satan has brought into the Church from the beginning under the pretended authority of the Spirit. Mohammed and the Pope have this religious principle in common, that scripture does not contain the perfection of doctrine, but that something higher has been revealed by the Spirit. The Anabaptists and Libertines have in our own day drawn their madness from the same ditch. But the spirit which introduced any invention foreign to the gospel is a deceiver and not of Christ; for Christ promises the Spirit who will confirm the teaching of the gospel as if he were signing it.

John II, p. 88

23 Scripture and the Church

A most pernicious error widely prevails that scripture has only so much weight as is conceded to it by the consent of the Church. As if the eternal and inviolable truth of God depended upon the decision of men! For they mock the Holy Spirit when they ask: Who can convince us that these writings came from God? Who can assure us that scripture has come down whole and intact even to our own day? Who can persuade us to receive one book in reverence but to exclude another, unless the Church prescribe a sure rule for all these matters? What reverence is due to scripture and what books ought to be reckoned within its canon depend, they say, upon the determination of the Church. Thus these sacriligious men, wishing to impose an unbridled

tyranny under cover of the Church, do not care about ensnaring
themselves and others in absurdities provided that they can force this
one notion upon the simple-minded: that the Church has authority in
all things.

Institutes I, vii, 1

24 Natural law

If the Gentiles by nature have the justice of God engraved upon their
minds, we surely cannot say they are utterly blind as to the conduct of
life. There is nothing more common than for a man to be sufficiently
instructed in a right standard of conduct by natural law. . . . Natural
law is that apprehension of the conscience which distinguishes sufficiently between just and unjust, and which deprives men of the excuse
of ignorance, while it proves them guilty by their own testimony.

Institutes II, ii, 22

25 Revealed divine law

It will not be difficult to decide the purpose of the whole law: the fulfilment of righteousness to form human life to the model of divine purity.
For God has so depicted his character in the law that if any man carries
out in deeds whatever is commanded there, he will express the image of
God in his own life. . . . It would be a mistake for anyone to think that
the law teaches only the rudiments and preliminaries of righteousness
by which men are introduced to good works without being guided to
them as their ultimate objective. . . . For where will anyone wish to go
who will not be satisfied by being taught to fear God, to worship
spiritually, to obey the commandments, to follow the righteous way of
the Lord, and to have a pure conscience, sincere faith and love? From
this is confirmed that interpretation of the law which seeks to find in the
law all the duties of piety and love.

Institutes II, viii, 51

26–8 Covenant

The Old Testament was established upon the free mercy of God and
was confirmed by Christ's intercession. For the gospel too declares

nothing else than that sinners are justified apart from their own merit by God's fatherly kindness; and the whole of it is summed up in Christ. Who then dares to separate the Jews from Christ, since, with them, we hear, was made the covenant of the gospel, the sole foundation of which is Christ? Who dares to estrange from the gift of free salvation those to whom we hear the doctrine of the righteousness of faith was imparted?

Institutes II, x, 4

27

Let us pass on to the formula of the covenant itself. This will not only satisfy calm spirits but will also demonstrate the ignorance of those who try to contradict it. For the Lord always covenanted with his servants thus: 'I will become your God and you shall become my people' (Leviticus 26, 12). The prophets also commonly explained that life and salvation and the whole of blessedness are embraced in these words.

Institutes II, x, 8

28

It is most evident that the covenant which the Lord once made with Abraham is no less in force today for Christians than it was of old for the Jewish people.

Institutes IV, xvi, 6

29   Christ – fulfilment of the law

The Pharisees had infected the people with a perverse opinion: that he who has committed nothing by way of outward works against the law fulfils the law. Christ reproves this most dangerous error and he declares a lascivious glance at a woman to be adultery (Matthew 5, 28). He testifies that 'anyone who hates his brother is a murderer' (I John 3, 15). . . . Those who did not understand his teaching, thought that Christ was another Moses, the giver of the law of the gospel which supplied what was lacking in the Mosaic law. . . . It is very easy to refute this error. They thought that Christ added to the law when he only restored it to its integrity, in that he freed and cleansed it when it

had been obscured by the falsehoods and defiled by the leaven of the
Pharisees.

Institutes II, viii, 7

30-1   Christ the mediator

Even if man had remained free from all stain, his condition would have
been too humble to reach God without a mediator. What, then of men
who are plunged into death and hell by their mortal ruin, defiled with
so many sins, tainted by so much corruption and overwhelmed with
every curse? In undertaking to describe the Mediator, St Paul with
good reason distinctly reminds us that he is man: 'One Mediator
between God and men, the man Jesus Christ' (I Timothy 2, 5).

Institutes II, xii, 1

31

We ought also to understand what we read in St Paul; after the judgement, 'Christ will deliver the Kingdom to his God and Father' (I
Corinthians 15, 24). . . . Until he comes forth as judge of the world
Christ will therefore reign, joining us to the Father as the measure of
our weakness permits. But when, as partakers in heavenly glory, we
shall see God as he is, Christ, having then discharged the office of
mediator, will cease to be the ambassador of his Father and will be
satisfied with that glory which he enjoyed before the creation of the
world.

Institutes II, vix, 3

D God's Merciful Justice

God's laws, covenant and the mediation of Christ were indispensable
to man's salvation because of his utter depravity. The 'bondage of the
will', as Luther had described man's inability to achieve anything that
was good, on his own, after the Fall of Adam became a major premiss
in Calvin's *Institutes* and, like Luther, he turned it into a relentless
critique of Erasmus and other humanists who had accepted man's

free-will.[1] The fall of Adam really happened and so did the fall of the angels to form devils and both had been foreseen by God. 'Justification by faith' was also to become for Calvin 'the main hinge upon which religion turns' (*Institutes* III, xi, 1). The space allotted to this fundamental notion indicates how essential it was to Calvin's theology. Faith represented the conviction, based upon scripture, reliant upon God's mercy, having Christ as its aim and the Holy Spirit as its agent, that we would be saved. God's mercy and favour – his grace – takes up the whole of the subject-matter of the third book of the *Institutes*. Through it alone can God's laws be fulfilled and by it alone can the believer be confident that the consequences of his sin will not remain with him. The conclusion follows for Calvin that those who are saved – the elect – are so entirely by God's free choice and it is by him that they are instructed. 'God effectively teaches his elect so that he may lead them to his grace'. Grace is not deserved by merit or by good deeds and comes because God appointed Christ as mediator for the salvation of mankind. The sacraments themselves do not impart grace, nor are they its vehicle but simply a sign of its conferment. 'The call is dependent upon election and accordingly is solely the work of grace'. This divine grace is common or general and available to all. At the same time it is special, bestowed through the Holy Spirit upon particular individuals to serve the divine purpose.

Divine providence, like the operation of grace, is universal and particular and shows its effects everywhere at all times. Calvin's comments on providence would be the point which led him inevitably towards the doctrine of predestination with which his name is most frequently associated. In fact, controversy about predestination had existed from as early as the fifth century when St Augustine had helped to bring about the condemnation of the Pelagians. The acceptance of the relatively small number of the saved as contrasted with the abundance of the damned was a commonplace in the Middle Ages. Calvin's teaching on the subject was an integral – but not a dominant – part of the *Institutes*. He was the first to accept that this was a difficult subject which could easily mislead and on which it was easy to be misinterpreted. But he insisted that, if some were the elect or saints, then it was inevitable that others were the reprobate or damned. He refused to accept that this was either a gloomy or a harsh notion for no one knew for sure whether he was saved or damned and those who

---

[1] E.G. Rupp and Benjamin Drewery, *Martin Luther* (London, 1970), section E.

persisted in despairing of God's grace were merely confirming for themselves in their pessimism their own possible reprobation. Each individual should accept, rather, that he had a vocation, or calling, which God had predestined for him. The controversy over predestination reached its height in the early 1550s and led to Calvin's writing a detailed treatise to refute his critics in 1553. At the same time, the hostility with which Calvinism was received in certain parts of Europe led ·to the notion of the saints or elect being readily accepted by persecuted communities. By the time of the final edition of the *Institutes*, Calvin accepted that to be persecuted for righteousness's sake was one sign of election.

32-3 Original sin

The first man rebelled against God's authority, not only in allowing himself to be caught by the blandishments of the devil, but also by despising truth and turning to lies; . . . faithlessness opened the door to ambition, and ambition was the mother of rebellion, man casting off the fear of God and giving free play to his lusts.

Institutes II, i, 4

33

Scripture teaches that man was estranged from God through sin and is an heir to wrath, subject to the curse of eternal death, excluded from all hope of salvation, beyond every blessing of God, the slave of Satan, captive under the yoke of sin, destined finally for a fearful destruction and already involved in it.

Institutes II, xvi, 2

34-5 Justification by faith

Wherever there is sin, there also are the wrath and vengeance of God. Now he is justified who is reckoned in the condition not of a sinner, but of a righteous man; and for that reason, he stands acquitted before God's judgement seat while all sinners are condemned. If an innocent accused person be summoned before the judgement seat of an impartial judge, where he will be judged according to his innocence, he is said to be 'justified' before the judge. So the man is justified before God who, freed from the company of sinners, has God to witness and affirm his righteousness. For justification is separated from works, not so that no good works may be done, or that what is done may be denied to be good, but that we may not rely upon them, glory in them, or ascribe salvation to them.

Institutes III, xi, 2

35

The sinner, received into communion with Christ, is reconciled to God by his grace, while, cleansed by Christ's blood, he obtains forgiveness of sins, and clothed with Christ's righteousness just as if it were his own, he stands free from care before the heavenly judgement seat.

Institutes II, xvii, 8

36-8 Grace

Free will is nót sufficient to enable man to do good works, unless he is assisted by grace, indeed by special grace, which only the elect receive through regeneration.

Institutes II, ii, 6

37

We need the promise of grace which can testify to us that the Father is merciful; since we can approach him in no other way and upon grace alone can the heart of man have repose.

Institutes II, ii, 7

38

The schoolmen are doubly deceived because they call faith an assurance of conscience while waiting to receive from God the reward for merits, and because they interpret the grace of God not as the imputation of free righteousness but as the spirit helping in the pursuit of holiness. . . . When Augustine says anything clearly, Lombard[2] obscures it and if there was anything slightly contaminated in Augustine, he corrupts it.

Institutes III, xi, 15

39-40   Predestination and Foreknowledge

No one dares simply deny predestination, by which God adopts some to hope of life, and sentences others to eternal death. But our opponents, especially those who make foreknowledge its cause, envelop it in numerous petty objections. . . . When we attribute foreknowledge to God, we mean that all things always were, and perpetually remain, under his eyes, so that to his knowledge there is nothing future or past, but all things are present. And they are present in such a way that he not only conceives them through ideas . . . but he truly looks upon them and discerns them as things placed before him. And this foreknowledge is extended throughout the universe to every creature. We call predestination God's eternal decree, by which he determined with himself what he willed to become of each man. For all are not created in equal condition; rather, eternal life is foreordained for some, eternal damnation for others.

Institutes III, xxi, 5

40

The decree, I admit, is a fearful one; and yet it is impossible to deny that God foreknew what the end of man was to be before he created him, because he had so ordained by his decree. If anyone inveighs at this point against the foreknowledge of God, he does so rashly and thoughtlessly. Why indeed should the heavenly judge be blamed because he was not ignorant of what was to happen? If there is any just or plausible complaint it applies to predestination. It ought not indeed to seem ridiculous for me to say that God not only foresaw the fall of the first man and in him the ruin of his posterity, but also brought it about in accordance with his own will. For as it belongs to his wisdom to know

---

[2] Peter Lombard (*c.* 1100-60), author of the *Sentences*, the most common theological textbook in the medieval universities.

beforehand everything that is to happen, so it belongs to his power to rule and direct everything by his hand.

Institutes II, xxxii, 7

41 Predestination and election

In actual fact, the covenant of life is not preached equally amongst all men, and amongst those to whom it is preached it does not gain the same acceptance either constantly or in equal degree. In this diversity, the wonderful depth of God's judgement is made known to us. For there is no doubt that this variety also serves the decision of God's eternal election. . . . This seems a baffling question to men. For they think nothing more inconsistent than that out of the common multitude of men some should be predestined to salvation, others to destruction. But it will become clear that they are needlessly entangled . . . for we shall never be clearly persuaded, as we ought to be, that our salvation flows from the wellspring of God's free mercy until we come to know his eternal election, which illumines God's grace by this contrast: that he does not indiscriminately adopt all into the hope of salvation but gives to some what he denies to others.

Institutes III, xxi, 1

As scripture clearly shows, we say that God established by his eternal and unchangeable plan those whom he long before determined once for all to receive into salvation, and those whom, on the other hand, he would devote to destruction. We assert that, with respect to the elect, this plan was founded upon his freely given mercy without regard to human worth; but, by his just and irreprehensible judgement, he has barred the door of life to those whom he has given over to damnation.

Institutes III, xxi, 7

42 Calling or vocation

Calvin's conception of vocation was widely adopted in protestant 'conduct books' and homilies during the succeeding century. Calvin conceived of it in a theological rather than moral or social sense.

The Lord bids each one of us in all life's actions to look to his calling. For he knows what restlessness human nature flames, what fickleness carries it here and there, how its ambition longs to embrace various things at once. Therefore, lest through our own stupidity and rashness, everything is turned topsy turvy, he has appointed duties for every man in his particular way of life. And so that no one may thoughtlessly transgress his limits, he has named these various kinds of living 'callings'. Therefore each individual has his own kind of living assigned to him by the Lord as a sort of sentry post, so that he may not heedlessly wander about throughout life. . . . It is enough if we know that the Lord's calling is in everything the beginning and foundation of well-doing.

Institutes III, x, 6

43   The reprobate

The reprobate wish to be considered excused in their sin on the grounds that they cannot avoid the necessity of sinning, especially since this sort of necessity is cast upon them by God's ordaining. But we deny that they are thus excused, because the ordinance of God, by which they complain that they are destined to destruction, has its own equity – unknown, indeed, to us, but very sure. From this we conclude that the ills they bear are all inflicted upon them by God's most righteous judgement.   Accordingly, we teach that they act perversely who seek out the source of their condemnation, turn their eyes to the hidden sanctuary of God's plan and wink at the corruption of nature from which it really springs.

Institutes II, xxxiii, 9

44   Persecution a special mark of God's favour

To suffer persecution for righteousness's sake is a singular comfort. For it ought to occur to us how much honour God bestows upon us with the special badge of his soldiers. . . . Let us not grieve or be troubled in thus far devoting our efforts to God, or count ourselves miserable in those matters in which he has with his own lips declared us blessed (Matthew 5, 10). Even poverty, if it be judged in itself, is misery; likewise exile, contempt, prison, disgrace; finally, death itself is the

THE INSTITUTES OF THE CHRISTIAN RELIGION

ultimate of all calamities. But when the favour of our God breathes upon us, every one of these things turns into happiness for us. We ought accordingly to be content with the testimony of Christ rather than with the false estimation of the flesh.

Institutes II, viii, 7

45 Providence

And truly God claims, and would have us grant him, omnipotence – not the empty, idle and almost unconscious sort . . . but a watchful, effective, active sort, engaged in ceaseless activity. . . . But if God's governance is so extended to all his works, it is a childish cavill to restrict it within the stream of nature. Indeed, those do much to defraud God of his glory and themselves of a profitable doctrine who confine God's providence to such narrow limits as though he allowed all things by a free course to be borne along according to a universal law of nature. For nothing would be more miserable than man if he were exposed to every movement of the sky, air, earth and waters. Besides, in this way God's particular goodness towards each one would be too unworthily reduced.

Institutes I, xvi, 3

46 Against astrology

Calvin was aware that some of the appeal and even the language (for instance that of 'election') was shared with the immensely popular Renaissance science of astrology. He wrote a treatise in 1549 against astrology and he repeated his scepticism of it in the *Institutes*.

The prophet forbids God's children 'to fear the stars and signs of heaven, as disbelievers commonly do' (Jeremiah 10, 2). Surely he does not condemn every sort of fear. But when unbelievers transfer the government of the universe from God to the stars they fancy that their bliss or their misery depends upon the decrees and indications of the stars, not upon God's will; so it comes about that their fear is transferred from him, towards whom alone they ought to direct it, to stars and comets. Let him, therefore, who would beware of this infidelity ever remember that there is no erratic power, nor action, nor motion in creatures, but that they are governed by God's secret plan in such a

way that nothing happens except what is knowingly and willingly
decreed by him.

Institutes I, xvi, 3

E Sacraments

The proper administration of the sacraments was for Calvin a proof of
the existence of a true Church through which alone they could be
dispensed. He preferred the term 'mystery' as the proper translation of
the Greek term for sacrament and regarded it as a sign or token of
God's grace. What the minister showed and attested by outward
forms, God accomplished within the believer's heart. For Calvin, there
were only two sacraments with biblical authority – those of baptism
and the Lord's Supper.

Baptism, whether by sprinkling or immersion, was a sign of forgiveness and of acceptance among the believers. Faith was its essential
accompaniment. It should properly be administered by a minister and
before witnesses for it was not a meaningless formula whose mere
repetition sufficed for its acceptance but it could and should be
bestowed upon children as early as possible. Of itself, it guaranteed
nothing – God had already decided upon election or reprobation; it
was simply a sign of acceptance within the Church. It was well attested
by biblical commands and precedents, especially since Calvin saw it as
replacing the circumcision of the old Mosaic law, a point which was
emphasized against the Anabaptists who found insufficient biblical
warranty for infant baptism. Calvin set no special value upon a set
form of words provided that they were clearly understood and that the
ceremony did not become 'a mere sound, a magic incantation' which
would be superstition at its worst. The principle to be followed was that
of a simple and literal obedience to the biblical injunctions avoiding the
superfluous and unnecessary innovations of the Roman rite.

The Lord's Supper was, like baptism, a necessity for all true
Christians. As an earthly father provides food for his family, so the
heavenly Father offered his children the spiritual food of the body and
blood of Christ. Calvin was acutely aware of the eucharistic controversy which had divided Luther from Zwingli[3] and he set out his own
convictions with the care and subtlety of the trained lawyer as well as

[3] G.R. Potter, *Huldrych Zwingli* (London, 1978), pp. 89–108.

the strong feeling of the evangelist. Transubstantiation, 'unknown to those better ages when the purer doctrine of religion still flourished' (*Institutes* IV, xiv, 17), he completely rejected. It was tantamount to the practising of magic upon the altar. The bread and wine remained bread and wine, symbolic of Christ's presence. Nor would he accept Luther's teaching that Christ was 'in, with and under' the bread. His own view of the eucharist came closer to that of Zwingli but it was not identical as was apparent in the long discussions which led to the agreement at Zurich in 1549 (*see below* part VII). Faith was indispensable and this, in turn, was strengthened by the sacrament. Participation with Christ in the eucharist became a reality in that the Holy Spirit brought Christ into the heart of the true believer, or, equally, lifted the heart of the believer to Christ in heaven. It was also 'a secret too sublime for my mind to understand or words to express. I experience it rather than understand it' (*Institutes* IV, xvii, 32). Calvin vigorously rejected the treatment of the Supper as a sacrifice. The cup was not to be denied to laymen and private masses were worthless. Participation by the faithful in the eucharist was indispensable and persistently notorious sinners were to be denied access to the holy table until they had given demonstrable evidence of repentance and amendment of life (*see below* part IV). Calvin expressed his notions about the Holy Supper simply and clearly in a treatise on the subject published in 1541. The other sacraments accepted by the Roman Catholic Church – matrimony, ordination, confirmation, penance and extreme unction – were not accepted by Calvin but he examined each one of them in the light of the evidence of the Bible.

47–9   Definition of a sacrament

A simple and proper definition would be to say that it is an outward sign by which the Lord seals upon our consciences the promise of his good will towards us in order to sustain the weakness of our faith; and we in turn attest our reverence for him alike in his presence and in the presence of his angels as well as before men. Here is another briefer definition: one may call it a testimony of divine grace towards us, confirmed by an outer sign, with mutual attestation of our reverence for him. Whichever of these definitions you choose, it does not differ in meaning from that of Augustine who teaches that a sacrament is 'a visible sign of a sacred thing' or 'a visible form of an invisible grace'.

Institutes IV, xiv, 1

48

When we speak of sacraments, two things are to be considered, the sign and the thing itself. In baptism the sign is water, but the thing is the washing of the soul by the blood of Christ and the mortifying of the flesh. The institution of Christ includes these two things. Now if the sign appears often inefficacious and fruitless, this happens through the abuse of men, which does not take away the nature of the sacrament. Let us learn not to tear away the thing signified from the sign. We must at the same time beware of another evil, such as prevails among the papists; for as they do not make a distinction as they ought to do between the thing and the sign, they stop at the outward element, and on that fix their hope of salvation. Therefore the sight of the water takes away their thoughts of the blood of Christ and the power of the Spirit. They do not regard Christ as the only author of all the blessings therein offered to us; they transfer the glory of his death to the water; they tie the secret power of the Spirit to the visible sign.

I *Peter*, p. 118

49

We may infer that in the sacraments the reality is given to us along with the sign; for when the Lord holds out a sacrament, he does not feed our eyes with an empty and unmeaning figure, but joins the truth with it, so as to testify that by means of this he acts upon us efficaciously. And this ought to be the more carefully observed, because there are few people in the present day who understand the true use of sacraments, and because many godly and learned men are engaged in frequent disputes about them.

First of all, we ought to believe that the truth must never be separated from the signs, though it ought to be distinguished from them. We perceive and feel a sign, such as the bread which is put into our hands by the minister in the Lord's Supper; and because we ought to seek Christ in heaven, our thoughts ought to be carried in that direction. By the hand of the minister he presents to us his body, that it may be actually enjoyed by the godly, who rise by faith to fellowship with him. He bestows it, therefore, on the godly, who raise their thoughts to him by faith; for he cannot deceive them.

Unbelievers indeed receive the sign; but because they linger in the world, and do not arrive at Christ's heavenly kingdom they have no experience of the truth; for he who has not faith cannot raise his thoughts to God, and therefore cannot partake of Christ.

Isaiah, p. 211

50 Baptism

Infants are not to be excluded from the kingdom of heaven merely because they happen to depart this present life before they have been immersed in water. . . . The children of believers are baptized not in order that, though formerly strangers to the Church, they may become for the first time children of God, but rather that, because of the blessing of the promise that they belonged already to the body of Christ they are received into the Church with this solemn sign.

Institutes IV, xv, 22

51 Against Anabaptists

As Christ orders them to teach before baptizing, and only wishes believers to be received for baptism, baptism appears not to be rightly administered unless faith has preceded it. On this pretext, the Anabaptists have raised a great tumult against infant baptism. . . . Those who by faith have come into the Church of God are, we see, to be counted his own stock, among the members of Christ, and likewise called to the inheritance of salvation. Nor is baptism in this way separated from faith or doctrine, for though infant children do not yet perceive, because of their age, the grace of God by faith, God includes them when he encourages their parents. So I deny that baptism is unwisely conferred on infants; the Lord calls them to it for he promises that he will be their God.

Gospel Harmony III, pp. 252–3

52–3 Spiritual presence in the Eucharist

So as we have . . . stated, from the physical things set forth in the sacrament, we are led to spiritual things by a kind of analogy. Thus, when bread is given as a symbol of Christ's body, we must at once grasp this comparison: as bread nourishes, sustains, and keeps the life of our body, so Christ's body is the only food to invigorate and enliven our soul. When we see wine set forth as a symbol of blood, we must reflect on the benefits which wine imparts to the body, and so realize that the same are spiritually imparted to us by Christ's blood.

Institutes IV, xvii, 3

53

I am not happy with those persons who, whilst recognizing that we have some communion with Christ, when asked to show what it is, make us partakers of the Spirit only, omitting mention of flesh and blood. As though all these things were said in vain: that his flesh is truly food, that his blood is truly drink (John 6, 55); that none shall have life except those who eat his flesh and drink his blood (John 6, 53), and other passages upon the same lines. . . . Rather I urge my readers not to confine their mental horizons too narrowly but to strive much higher than I can lead them. For, whenever this matter is discussed, when I have tried to say everything, I feel that I have yet said little in proportion to its worth. And although my mind can think beyond what my tongue can utter, yet even my mind is defeated and overwhelmed with the greatness of the thing. Therefore, nothing remains but to break forth in wonder at this mystery, which plainly neither the mind is able to conceive nor the tongue to express.

Institutes IV, xvii, 7

54   Against the adoration of the sacraments

Those who have devised the adoration of the sacraments have not only dreamed it up by themselves apart from scripture, where no mention of it can be found . . . but also, with scripture crying out against it [idolatry], they have forsaken the living God and fashioned a God after their own desire. For what is idolatry if not this: to worship the gifts in place of the Giver himself? . . .

They devised rites utterly alien to the institution of the Supper, with the intention of paying divine honours to the sign. . . . What is their pretext for their boast that they worship Christ in that bread, when they have no promise of any such thing? They consecrate the host, as they call it, to carry about in procession, to display it in solemn spectacle that it may be seen, worshipped and called upon. I ask by what power they think it duly consecrated. To be sure, they will bring forward these words: 'This is my body'. But I object, on the contrary, that at the same time this was said: 'Take and eat'. . . . For when a promise is joined to a command, I say that the latter is included in the former, so that, separated from it, it becomes no promise at all.

Institutes IV, xvii, 36–7

55 How to celebrate the Lord's Supper

To remove this great pile of ceremonies, the Supper could be administered most becomingly if it were set before the church very often, and at least once a week. First, then, it should begin with public prayers. After this a sermon should be given. Then, when bread and wine have been placed on the table, the minister should repeat the words of institution of the Supper. Next, he should recite the promises which were left to us in it: at the same time, he should excommunicate all who are debarred from it by the Lord's prohibition. Afterwards, he should pray that the Lord, with the kindness wherewith he has bestowed this sacred food upon us, also teach and form us to receive it with faith and thankfulness of heart, and, inasmuch as we are not so of ourselves, by his mercy make us worthy of such a feast. But here, either psalms should be sung or something be read, and in becoming order the believers should partake of the most holy banquet. When the Supper is finished, there should be an exhortation to sincere faith and confession of faith, to love and behaviour worthy of Christians. At the end, thanks should be given and praises sung to God. When these things are finished, the church should be dismissed in peace.

Institutes IV, xvii, 43

56 Marriage not a sacrament

[Marriage] is a good and holy ordinance of God: agriculture, architecture, shoemaking and hairdressing are lawful ordinances of God, but they are not sacraments. For in a sacrament the essential requirement is not only that it is a work of God but also an outward ceremony

appointed by God to confirm a promise. Even children can see that
there is no promise of the sort in matrimony.

Institutes IV, xix, 34

57 Ordination of ministers

Calvin readily accepted the ritual of the 'laying on of hands' since both the Old
and New Testaments gave it scriptural authority. Ordination was a public
acknowledgement of a divine call to the individual concerned, but it was not,
however, a sacrament. The service did not bring or confer anything that was
not there already. Any baptized male could become a minister and he was
maintained by his congregation without any difference in status. He was
provided at ordination with no miraculous powers, no 'indelible stigma'.
Calvin thought that the elaborate ordination ceremonial of the medieval
Church represented a departure from the practices of the apostles and an
attempt to increase the power of the hierarchical Roman Catholic Church.

It is clear that when the apostles admitted any man to the ministry, they
used no other ceremony than the laying-on of hands. I judge that this
rite derived from the custom of the Hebrews who, as it were, presented
to God by the laying on of hands that which they wished to be blessed
and consecrated. . . . Although there exists no set precept for the
laying on of hands, because we see it in continual use with the apostles,
their very careful observance ought to serve in lieu of a precept. And
surely it is useful for the dignity of the ministry to be commended to the
people by this sort of sign, as also to warn the one ordained that he is no
longer a law unto himself, but bound in servitude to God and the
Church. Moreover, it will be no empty sign if it is restored to its own
true origin. For if the Spirit of God establishes nothing without cause in
the Church, we should feel that this ceremony, since it has proceeded
from him, is not useless, provided that it is not turned to superstitious
abuse.

Institutes IV, iii, 16

58–60 Penance

Calvin objected to the forced auricular confession which had become a
required sacrament in the Roman Catholic Church from the time of Innocent
III and the Fourth Lateran Council (1215), and the exclusive sacerdotal claims
to absolution that went with it. The idea of the repentance which such

absolution produced was wholly unconvincing. Instead, Calvin thought that there was a place for general confession by a congregation; notorious and scandalous individual faults might suitably call for public recognition and evidence of contrition. That a person should seek advice and help from his minister to whom he would 'confess' was entirely desirable, but this was quite different from the mandatory penitential system of the Roman Catholic Church.

There has always been great strife between the canon lawyers and the scholastic theologians concerning confession. The latter contend that confession is enjoined by divine precept; the former claim that it is commanded only by ecclesiastical constitutions. . . .

But I marvel how shamelessly our opponents dare contend that the confession of which they speak is divinely ordained. Of course we admit that its practice is very ancient, but we can easily prove that it was formerly free. Surely, even their records declare that no law or constitution concerning it had been set up before the time of Innocent III. Surely, if they had had a more ancient law than those, they would have seized upon it, rather than, content with the decree of the Lateran Council, make themselves ridiculous even to children.

Institutes III, iv, 4, 7

59

The doctrine taught by the scholastics in later times is somewhat worse. . . . For they are so doggedly set in outward exercises that you gather nothing else from their huge volumes than that repentance is a discipline and austerity that serves partly to tame the flesh, partly to chastise and punish faults. They are wonderfully silent concerning the inward renewal of the mind, which bears with it true correction of life. Among them there is, instead, much talk concerning contrition and attrition. They torture souls with many misgivings, and immerse them in a sea of troubles and anxiety. But where they seem to have wounded hearts deeply, they heal all the bitterness with a light sprinkling of ceremonies.

Institutes III, iv, 1

60

There is a place for the 'power of the keys' in the three following modes of confession – when the whole church in a solemn recognition of its defects asks for pardon; or when a private individual, who has given public offence by some notable transgression, expresses his repentance; or when some one on account of a troubled conscience needs the help of his minister and tells him of his difficulties. As regards reparation for the offence, the case is altered. For in this instance, in addition to peace of conscience the chief purpose is to remove hatred and reunite people in the bond of peace. . . . With regard to the ministry of the keys, its whole power consists in this, that the grace of the gospel is publicly and privately imprinted on the minds of the believers by means of those whom the Lord has appointed, and the only way this can be done is by preaching.

Institutes III, iv, 14

III Calvin in Exile

A Geneva

Following his departure from France, Calvin lived the rootless life of an exile. After more than a year in Basel, he went to join other French exiles (such as Clément Marot, the translator of the Psalms into metrical French poetry) at the court of Renée, duchess of Ferrara. Like her cousin at the court of Francis I, Marguerite of Navarre, Renée was a protector of those with advanced opinions. Her husband, Hercules II Borgia, duke of Ferrara, however, was a partisan of the Holy Roman Emperor Çharles V. The duke became alarmed at the growth of overt heretical opinions in his dukedom and began to persecute reformers in April 1536. Renée did her best to protect them but Calvin judged it prudent again to retire, once more to Basel. From there, he undertook a swift journey to Paris and Noyon to wind up his family affairs in France before a more severe edict against heretics made such a trip too dangerous for him. He had intended making his way direct to Strasbourg from France, but troop movement in that region caused him to make a detour which led him to Geneva. By chance, Calvin was recognized by the preacher there, Guillaume Farel, and persuaded, much against his inclination, to stay for a while and assist in the reformation of the city which, as it happened, had reached at that moment (August 1536) a delicate and confusing climax.

Geneva was an independent city of some 10,000 inhabitants. A survey of the property within the city's walls in 1537 shows that there were over a thousand buildings, 100 barns and 12 mills inside its recently constructed and rather menacing city walls. It was bigger than any other city in the nearby Swiss confederation although it was small in comparison with its cosmopolitan neighbour downstream along the Rhône, Lyons. Geneva's importance lay principally in its location on a series of political, linguistic and religious frontiers which put it in a kind of 'no-man's land' commanding communications between Savoy on the one hand and the Swiss confederation and parts of France and the Holy Roman Empire on the other (see map p. xiv). Geneva was originally an episcopal city, ruled by a bishop. The dukes of Savoy, however, whose territories neatly surrounded the city until 1536, gradually turned the bishopric into a family possession and the city into a satellite of their duchy. The *bourgeois* (old-established Genevan families) and the *habitants* (inhabitants who had newly migrated to the city) steadily increased their effective influence over their own affairs so that, by 1519, they had gained a substantial measure of self-government. This was exercised through four Syndics as chief officials and a complex but far from unique series of councils of which the most important was the small council of 24 (exclusively for the *bourgeois*). Other councils such as the council of 60, the council of 200 and the general council of the city occasionally met to debate and decide important issues and elections.

Loosely established factions, sometimes with their own badges, slogans and inns for meeting-places, made Genevan politics – like that of many other sixteenth-century cities – lively and unpredictable. The most divisive issue emerged clearly and suddenly in 1519 with a proposal that the city should sign an alliance of confederation (*combourgeoisie*) with the two neighbouring Swiss cantons of Berne and Freibourg. Michel Roset, secretary to the small council from 1555, later recalled in his chronicle the 'deliverance' of Geneva from papal tyranny and Savoyard overlordship and the appearance of the *Patriots* or *Confederates* (*Eidgenossen* or *Eigenots*) led by Philibert Berthelier against the *Mamelukes* (*Mamellus*), supporters of the duke of Savoy and the bishop of Geneva. In 1519, the leader of the *Eidgenossen* (the word is probably the etymological root for the term *Huguenot* in France) was executed and the authority of the bishop and duke was temporarily reasserted. In 1526, however, the *Eidgenossen* again seized control of the city councils and an alliance of *combourgeoisie* with Berne and Freibourg was promptly signed. The bishop and many canons in his chapter left the city to exile; some of the Savoyard and episcopal rights and property were confiscated by the municipality.

Over the next 10 years the duke and bishop were persistent and ingenious in trying to regain their hold on Geneva. They applied diplomatic pressure to members of the Swiss confederation against the city, appealed to the Emperor Charles V for help, and assisted the *sujets* (inhabitants of villages near Geneva who had owed allegiance to the bishop and now found themselves the subjects of the city of Geneva) to form a 'Confraternity of the Spoon' and to wage war on Genevan commerce and property. Armed contingents were also despatched to take Geneva but the newly-constructed city walls and the timely support of Berne prevented their gaining any victory. Eventually Berne 'liberated' the territories surrounding Geneva in Gex, Thonon and Ternier in 1536 and on 8 August 1536, when the Genevans heard that their treaty of confederation with Berne had been renewed on terms which assured their freedom, they recorded jubilantly that they were now 'as princes in our city'.

The Genevan reformation rode on the back of this political change. There were few Protestants noted in the city before 1532. The arrival of the preacher Guillaume Farel, provided with a passport from Berne, began the process which led to the first evangelical service being held on Good Friday 1533 in a garden where a French immigrant hat-maker distributed the Holy Supper.

In the course of the following three years when the dispute with the exiled bishop of Geneva and the duke of Savoy was at its height, the cause of the Reformation kept the city bitterly divided. As a result it lost one of the principal confederates (the Catholic canton of Freibourg), and witnessed some savage scenes of street-fighting between supporters of the various factions. It also suffered from icono-clastic destruction of religious images and forcible entry and despolia-tion of ecclesiastical property in the Upper City near the cathedral where the canons once lived. This was where for nearly two years Calvin was to stay with Guillaume Farel and to attempt to impose some disciplined reformation upon a city in turmoil.

61 Arrival in Geneva (August 1536)

Calvin gave his own account of his fortuitous arrival in his preface to his *Commentary upon the Psalms* in 1557.

Wherever I went, I took care to conceal that I was the author of the *Institutes* and resolved to retain my privacy and obscurity. At length, Guillaume Farel[1] detained me in Geneva, not so much by counsel and exhortation, as by a dreadful threat which I felt in the same way as if

---

[1] Guillaume Farel (*c.* 1509–65), born in Dauphiné, studied in Paris under Lefèvre d'Etaples and subsequently preached the gospel in Paris, Meaux and in Dauphiné before retiring to Switzerland where, following his efforts, many towns were reformed. He later became minister in Neuchâtel.

God had laid his mighty hand upon me from heaven to arrest me. As the most direct road to Strasbourg, to which I then intended to retire, was shut by the wars, I decided to go quickly via Geneva, not intending to spend longer than a single night in the city. A little before this, popery had been driven from the place by the exertions of that excellent man whom I have just mentioned and Pierre Viret.[2] But matters were not yet settled there and the city was divided into ungodly and dangerous factions. Then a person . . . discovered who I was and made me known to the rest. Upon this, Farel, who was consumed with an extraordinary zeal to advance the gospel, immediately strained every nerve to detain me. And, after learning that my heart was set upon devoting myself to private studies, for which I wished to keep myself free from other pursuits, and, finding that he achieved nothing by his entreaties, he proceeded to warn me that God would curse my retirement and the tranquillity which I sought for my studies if I withdrew and refused to help when it was so urgently needed. By this I was so struck with terror that I gave up the journey I had planned to undertake. But, aware of my natural shyness, I refused to tie myself to any particular position.

CR XXXIX, cols. 23–6

62   Geneva's factions (1519)

Amongst others, the person principally noticed by the bishop was Philibert Berthelier, a great entrepreneur amongst the city's inhabitants, whose freedoms became his battlecry. Finding himself constrained in Geneva, he left for Freibourg where he had already been made a *bourgeois* of that city. He raised the question there of the infringements that were occurring upon the liberties of Genevans. . . .

Those who had hitherto acquired the status of *bourgeois* at Freibourg [in Geneva] solicited others to join them at dinners and arranged other meetings when they agreed upon their demands. . . . Thus 60 people were enrolled and despatched to Freibourg to ask for a confederation and they were granted it provided that it was consented to generally in Geneva. They then became more open in their activities, assembling in larger numbers and calling the supporters of the duke *Mamellus*, or

---

[2] Pierre Viret (1511–71), born at Orbe in Switzerland, educated in Paris, arrived in Geneva in 1534 and later became one of Calvin's close friends.

those who renounced liberty, and sometimes *Monseigneuristes*. They were called in their turn *Eugenos* by the *Mamellus* because they were known to be bound by an oath or *Eidgnossen*. This division was a deep one and lasted for a long time so that the *Eugenos* became stronger in the number of voices on their side. Their sign was a cross tied in their belts. M. Roset, *Sommaire recueil de ce qui se trouve des affaires de Genève et de l'estat de l'église en icelle iusques à l'an 1562* in *les Chroniques de Genève* (ed. H. Fazy, Geneva, 1894) pp. 77, 86-7

63 The Confraternity of the Spoon

The alliance between the three cities [Berne, Freibourg and Geneva] was solemnly ratified in a general council on Monday 12 March 1526 and, on the same morning, the bishop left the city so as not to be present. . . .

[1528] It was rumoured that the duke promised 12,000 men to the bishop to assist him to overcome the citizens who wanted to overthrow all forms of princely authority. On 18 March a man from Geneva was killed on the bridge over the river Arve by ducal supporters with an arquebus. The court at Vienna excommunicated the city, and those around it were notified of the fact. . . .

[1528-9] However, the subjects [*sujets* - see p. 44] formed a conspiracy called the Gentlemen of the Spoon because their leaders dined and ate together upon rice with a spoon, and each of them took it as a sign of their confraternity and so did other gentlemen of Savoy who wanted to join the plot. The most daring amongst them said that they wanted to spoon Geneva up. They assembled in arms numerous times . . . and held the town under threat of a general mobilization.

Roset, *Sommaire recueil*, pp. 113, 129

64 The beginnings of the Reformation in Geneva

A letter from Guillaume Farel in Geneva to his friend in Strasbourg, Martin Bucer, 22 October 1533.

The people of Geneva have taken to the Word with the most praiseworthy zeal. They have been joined by Fortunat,[3] but not in the position of a minister of religion, since the supporters of the Pope have

[3] The name taken by a former monk in Geneva, Andronius Andry.

decided that there shall be no controversial preaching on either side.
All the same, people are allowed to speak openly about Christ in
private houses and in the streets provided they do not attempt to preach
sermons. If some use this opportunity to urge people towards religion
so much the better. May Christ bring growth and advancement to this
Church; with his help may it continue in holiness, when the numerous
opponents who prevent this have been overcome.

> Quoted in H. Naef, *Origines de la réforme à
> Genève* (Geneva, 1936) II, p. 463

65   Geneva's acceptance of reform

Minutes of the council of 24 in Geneva, 10 March 1536
Guillaume Farel urged that the Word of God should be preached to the
villages under Genevan jurisdiction. It was agreed that a general
proclamation should be read out in each of them urging the people to
obedience, abstinence from sin and from blasphemy.

Minutes of the council of 24, 24 March 1536
It was also agreed that, in order to encourage civic unity, every quarter
of the city should be told that it was forbidden henceforth to go and hear
Catholic mass outside the city walls.

Minutes of the council of 200, 21 May 1536
The general council was summoned to the cloister by bell and trumpet
according to custom. The syndic Claude Savoye proposed the changes
and, following that, those who were against them were asked to speak
and explain why they did not wish to live according to the scriptures
and God's holy Word such as had been preached daily in the city since
the abolition of masses, images and other papal abuses. Since only one
person spoke against it, it was generally agreed by a show of hands and
a promise before God that we should live in future according to his
holy, evangelical laws and by the Word of God, and that we should
abandon all masses and other ceremonies and papal abuses and everything which is attached to them. It was also unanimously agreed that
someone of requisite knowledge should be employed to teach in a
school without charging any fees and, in addition, that all parents
should be required to send their children to school and make them
learn there.

> *CR* XL, cols. 201–2

B Deposition from Geneva (April 1538)

Although Calvin accepted no official position as minister, there is every indication that he and Guillaume Farel co-operated closely in Geneva from August 1536 until their enforced exclusion from the city in April 1538. These 18 months provide a model of the difficulties which had been already experienced in numerous cities in the course of the Reformation.

Their first task was to produce a kind of 'new covenant', a 'confession of faith, which all the citizens and inhabitants of Geneva . . . must promise to accept and hold to'. This was duly presented to the council of 24 on 10 November 1536 and accepted by them. This was followed by a series of proposed articles for the government of the Church which were debated in January 1537 and accepted with some modifications. These were to become the blueprint for Calvin's *Ecclesiastical Ordinances* for Geneva of November 1541 (*see below* part IV).

Acceptance of these measures and their enforcement upon a bitterly divided city was, however, the preachers' real problem. As Beza's *Life of Calvin* records, they had some initial successes, for the city magistrates eventually subscribed to the confession themselves and Calvin and Farel received their support in a large public debate held with two itinerant Anabaptists. But by November 1537 it was clear that the public swearing of oaths to uphold the confession was bitterly dividing the city. The German and pro-Berne merchants of the *rue des Allemands* refused to conform, and there were clear signs that factions were growing up for and against the preachers as they had done for and against the bishop 10 years previously. Some took their stand upon the somewhat Anabaptist grounds that swearing to observe a purely human document was perjury, and at a public meeting on 6 November Calvin explained that what was involved was a solemn oath to keep the faith of God – in fact a renewal of the covenant with God.

In the following year, opinion turned rapidly against Farel and Calvin. In February the city elections produced four new syndics who were suspicious of the French preachers and determined that the magistrates alone should decide religious policy. The canton of Berne held a synod at Lausanne beginning on 31 March 1538 to produce religious uniformity amongst the various evangelical Churches in its confederation. The magistrates wanted Geneva's preachers to accept the decisions of this synod, but Calvin and Farel refused and were asked to leave the city immediately after Easter. Following a fruitless attempt to persuade Berne to mediate on their behalf, Calvin and Farel undertook a wet and miserable journey to Basel without possessions, books or employment.

66   First steps to settle Geneva's Reformation

At this time, Calvin published a short formula of Christian doctrine, adapted to the Church of Geneva. . . . To this he added a catechism, not the one that we now have in the form of question and answer, but another much shorter one, containing only the leading heads of religion. Endeavouring afterwards with Farel and Courault[4] to settle the affairs of the Church, Calvin's first objective was to obtain from the citizens, at a meeting attended by the whole city, an open abjuration of the papacy, and an oath of adherence to the Christian religion and its discipline, as comprehended under a few headings. Most of Calvin's colleagues kept aloof from this struggle through timidity and some of them, to his great unease, even secretly impeded the work of the Lord. As was to be expected in a city which had just been delivered from the snares of the duke of Savoy and the yoke of Antichrist, and in which factions still greatly prevailed, some citizens refused to take the oath but, by the good hand of the Lord, on 20 July 1537 (the clerk of the city taking a leading part) the senate and people of Geneva solemnly declared their adherence to the leading doctrines and discipline of the Christian religion. Satan, exasperated (but in vain) at these proceedings . . . stirred up the Anabaptists first. . . . But, as the event showed, the Lord had anticipated Satan. For Calvin and his colleagues, having brought the Anabaptists to a free discussion in public, so thoroughly refuted them by the Word of God alone on 18 March 1537 that, afterwards, only one or two appeared in that church – a rare instance of success.[5]

CR XLIX, col. 126

[4] Augustin Courault (?–1538), an elderly, blind monk who had previously preached the Reformation in Paris before joining Farel in Geneva.

[5] A reference to a public disputation in the college de Rive on 16 March 1537 with Herman of Gerbehaye and Andrew Benoît of Engelen, two Anabaptists from Flanders. Herman later recanted his Anabaptism before Calvin in Strasbourg.

67   Lack of support for the confession

Register of the council of 24 (12 November 1537)
It was reported that yesterday the people who had not yet made their
oaths to the Reformation were asked to do so, street by street; whilst
many came, many others did not do so. No one came from the *rue des
Allemands*. It was decided that they should be commanded to leave the
city if they did not wish to make a confession to the reformation.

26 November 1537
Some people have been reported as thinking that it was perjury to
swear to a confession which had been dictated to them in writing.
[Farel or Calvin] . . . replied that if the contents of the written confession were studied carefully it would be seen that this was not the case. It
was a confession made according to God. Examples from holy scripture proved (in Nehemiah and Jeremiah) that the people should be
gathered together and should swear to hold to faith in God and to his
commandments. It was also said that the latest messengers from Berne
agreed that it was perjury to swear to an oath like this.

Register of the council of 200, 14 December 1537
Guillaume Farel and Calvin explained how they had journeyed to
Berne because some people there believed that it was perjury to swear
an oath to the confession. They said that Berne had decided to send
some investigators to see if the affair had been properly and truly
managed. It has now come to pass that, as a result of some other
comments, they have been dissuaded from sending any investigators
and have written again to us. In this and other letters from Berne, it
was reported that our preachers had taught from the pulpit that all evils
come from Germany.

2 January 1538
It was reported that slanderous remarks were spreading around the
town against the preachers. It was decided that the matters should be
passed on to the lieutenant for investigation and prosecution.

16 January 1538
It was said that many people in and around the city repeated slogans
which divided the city and that these originated with some drunkards
who went about the town at night from one tavern to another saying,
'You are brothers in Christ', and other similar phrases mocking the

preachers. It was decided that an investigation should be conducted
into this.

CR XLIX, cols. 216–22

68   Synod of Lausanne and the exile of Calvin and Farel

Register of the general council of the city, 23 April 1538
A general council of the city has been proposed to agree that every one
should live according to the ceremonies agreed upon lately at
Lausanne where the preachers Farel and Calvin had been in
attendance. Three letters that it was proposed should be sent to Berne
were read out. It was the majority opinion that they wanted to live
according to the ceremonies agreed at Lausanne recently and to accept
the decrees of that synod.

It was also proposed that, if Calvin, Farel and any other preacher did
not wish to obey the orders of the magistrates then it was a question
whether they should continue in their posts which the general council
and the small council should vote upon. The majority opinion was in
favour of giving them the next three days to leave the town.

Register of the council of 24, 23 April 1538
M. de Soultier was sent to order Master Guillaume Farel and Calvin to
preach no longer in the city and leave it within three days, as had been
agreed at the general meeting. The preachers replied (with Calvin
speaking for them), when they heard this, by saying 'Very well, so be
it. If we had laboured for men, we would have been badly rewarded.
But we serve a great Lord who will recompense us.'

CR XLIX, cols. 226–7

69   Journey to Basel (May 1538)

To Pierre Viret
We have at length reached Basel, well soaked with the rain and completely exhausted and worn out. Nor was the journey without danger
for, in fact, one of us was almost carried away by the swollen waters.
But we have experienced more tender treatment from the impetuous
river than from our fellow-men.

CR XXXVIII, cols. 201–2

C Strasbourg

Calvin's exile from Geneva affected him deeply. His letters betray the extent to which it had hurt him; he had believed that he had a divine calling to be a preacher and providence seemed to have decreed otherwise. Fortunately, the minister in Strasbourg, Martin Bucer, invited Calvin to go to Strasbourg to become a minister to the small church of exiled Frenchmen in the city and undertake some lecturing in theology at the university. After initial misgivings, Calvin accepted the responsibility. It was a vital period for his development. Over the period of the next three years, Calvin greatly increased his friendships amongst the reformed theologians of Switzerland and Germany. He wrote a great deal, producing a new edition of the *Institutes* and a French translation of it, as well as his first biblical commentary (the letters of St Paul to the Romans). He married Idolette de Bure, formerly a wife to an Anabaptist, and also became aware in the more tolerant and cosmopolitan atmosphere of Strasbourg of the extent of Anabaptist sympathies in Europe. Above all, Calvin learnt from Bucer's Strasbourg about the operation of a consistory and the discipline of a reformed community within a large city and this was to be invaluable to him when he returned to Geneva.

Calvin was exceedingly reluctant to leave Strasbourg when he was eventually invited to return to Geneva in 1541. He was aware that the bitterness of the factional struggles within the city had increased since his departure and that his successors as preachers in the city had also left it in despair. He felt responsible to his congregation in Strasbourg and did not wish to step back to Geneva without Guillaume Farel. Complicated negotiations eventually secured Calvin's release from Strasbourg for an initial period of not longer than six months. He was escorted back to the city by Genevan escorts and given a well-furnished lodging in the *rue des chanoines* with a good monthly salary. Although Calvin never felt entirely at ease in Geneva, he stayed there for the rest of his life and his days as an exile were effectively over.

70   Invitation to Strasbourg

Calvin's own memories of the event were recalled in the preface to his commentary upon the Psalms (1557).

I was not sustained by such greatness of mind as not to rejoice more

than became me when, in consequence of such commotions, I was
banished from Geneva. By this means, having been set at liberty and
loosened from the tie of my vocation, I resolved to live a private life,
free from the burdens and cares of any public office until that most
excellent servant of Christ, Martin Bucer, employing a similar kind of
remonstration to me as that to which Farel had had recourse before,
drew me to a new office. . . . Alarmed by the example of Jonas which
he put before me, I continued in the work of teaching.

Psalms I, pp. 212–14

71 Straitened circumstances in Strasbourg

To Guillaume Farel, April 1539
From my books, which are still in Geneva, there will be enough to
satisfy my landlord until next winter; as to the future, the Lord will
provide. Although I had at one time a great many friends in France,
there was not one of them who offered me a farthing.

CR XXXVIII, col. 340

72 Search for a wife

To Guillaume Farel, 19 May 1539
Concerning marriage I shall now speak more plainly. . . . Always
bear in mind what I seek to find in her; for I am not one of those insane
lovers who embrace also the vices of those whom they love so that they
are smitten at first sight with a fine figure. The only sort of beauty
which attracts me is some one who is chaste, not too nice or fastidious,
economical, patient and some one who will (it is to be hoped) be concerned about my health. Therefore, if you think well of it, set out
immediately in case some one else gets there beforehand.

CR XXXVIII, col. 438

73 Friendship with Bullinger

Heinrich Bullinger (1504–75) was Zwingli's friend and successor as minister
in the church in Zurich. Calvin's letters to him from Strasbourg laid the
foundations for a lasting friendship between the two theologians.

To Bullinger, 12 March 1540

What ought we rather, my dear Bullinger, to be writing to each other about at this time rather than the preserving and confirming by every possible means within our power of brotherly kindness amongst ourselves? We see how much importance this carries, not only upon our own account, but for the sake of the whole body of professing Christians everywhere, so that all those to whom the Lord has given a personal charge in the ordering of his Church should agree together in a sincere and cordial understanding.

CR XXXIX, col. 28

74 Calvin's first reactions to the invitation to return to Geneva

To Guillaume Farel, 27 October 1540

Whenever I remember the state of wretchedness in which I existed there, how can it be otherwise than that my soul should shudder at any proposal to return there? I pass entirely over that disquiet which perpetually tossed us up and down and, from the moment that I became your colleague, drove us from one side to the other. I know indeed from experience that wherever I turned I would find all kinds of irritations put in my way. I know too that if I want to live by Christ this world must be to me a scene of trail and vexation, for the present life is a field of combat. At the same time, whilst I remind myself of the torture that my conscience went through at that time and how much anxiety I suffered continually, you will pardon me if I dread that place as having something of a fatality attached to it in my own case. You yourself and God are my best witnesses that no lesser tie would have sufficed to keep me there so long had I not been afraid to throw off the yoke of my calling which I was well assured had been laid upon me by the Lord. . . . Here at Strasbourg I have only to take charge of a few, and the majority come to hear me not so much as a pastor but as a professor, with due attention and reverence. You allege that I am too sensitive and, after having been covered with these flatteries, cannot now bear in patience to hear any harsher sounds. You will find yourself mistaken, however, if you allow yourself really to believe that. But when I find it arduous enough to superintend and oversee as I ought those few who may be called teachable and disciplined, how shall I ever be able to restrain and keep within due bounds so great a multitude?

CR XXXIX, cols. 91–2

75   Return to Geneva

Register of the council of Geneva (13 September 1541)
Master John Calvin, minister of the gospel. The same has arrived from Strasbourg, and has brought letters from Strasbourg and from its preachers, as well as from Basel, which have been read. Afterwards he made, at some length, his apologies for his delayed arrival. That done, he asked that the Church be set in order and a memorandum was drawn up to this effect. He also asked that councillors should be elected to have a liaison with the council over this. And, concerning himself, he offered himself as ever the servant of Geneva.

CR XLIX, col. 282

IV Calvin and Genevan Church Settlement

A Calvin and Politics

Calvin never wrote any formal treatise on government or politics and he took great care to stand aside from the purely political matters which divided the city on his return in 1541 and afterwards. However, his first task was to provide a series of laws, agreed by the magistrates and people of the city, under which the Genevan Church could exercise its authority. The *Institutes*, especially the last two sections of the original edition, provides important insights into the way Calvin approached this problem.

In a city where the word 'liberty' had been interpreted as freedom from the authority of the dukes of Savoy and episcopal control, Calvin was to introduce a different notion. For him, as for Luther, conscience lay at the heart of the question. A conscience freed from sin constituted the essence of true personal freedom. To disobey authority was no liberty but an offence against God's laws. Magistracy, as the French lawyers inevitably termed the exercise of authority, was a lawful and godly calling and to disobey it was therefore to disobey God. Unjust magistrates were to be obeyed because their cruelty was part of God's providence.

Before the *Institutes* was written, German Protestant lawyers and political theorists (notably in Hesse and Strasbourg) had already developed a coherent theory of a limited right to resist tyrannical authority. It rested on the authority and status of the lesser magistrates, the princes and imperial cities, in the German imperial constitution and it justified their revolt against the emperor, Charles V. Calvin took this a stage further in one significant passage in the *Institutes*. Here he permitted *elected* authorities (*populares magistratus*) a right to resist tyrants. Not to do so, indeed, would be against such magistrates' consciences, their duty and calling. The paragraph, it is true, is hedged with qualifications and Calvin's customary clarity disappears. But, at the time, it was suggestive and was reinforced by commentaries and sermons, delivered or printed towards the end of Calvin's life. When linked with covenant theology (*see above*, pp. 24–5) it enabled others, less cautious than Calvin was, to create a wider and more corrosive theory of the right to resist tyrannical authority within broadly Calvinist tenets (*see below*, sections VII and VIII).

Tyranny was, according to Calvin, an evil congenital to all political systems which were human and fallible unless supported by the hand of God. Nevertheless, Calvin expressed a clear preference for the lesser evil of a mixed government as against a monarchy. He was habitually severe in his judgement of kings, even those of recent memory. There is little doubt that his exile from France had placed him in cities whose system of government was the most congenial he could have found in sixteenth-century Europe.

76   Conscience and Christian liberty

As soon as any mention is made of Christian liberty, either inordinate passions rage, or violent emotions arise unless these wanton spirits are opposed in time, who otherwise most wickedly corrupt the best things. Some, on the pretext of this freedom, shake off all obedience towards God and break out into unrestrained licence. Others turn away from such liberty, thinking that it removes all moderation, order and choice of things. What should we do when surrounded by such perplexities? Should we say good-bye to Christian freedom, thus cutting off the risk from such dangers? But, as we have said, unless this freedom is properly understood, neither Christ nor the truth of his gospel, nor the inner peace of the soul can rightly be known. . . .

Christian freedom consists, in my opinion, of three propositions. The first, that the consciences of believers, in seeking assurance of their justification before God, should rise above and advance beyond the law, forgetting all the righteousness of the law. For since, as we have shown elsewhere, the law leaves no one righteous, either it excludes us from all hope of justification or we ought to be freed from it, and in such a way, indeed, that no account is taken of the good works we manage to achieve. . . .

The second part of Christian liberty, which is dependent upon the first, is that consciences observe the law, not as if constrained by the necessity of the law, but that, freed from the law's yoke, they willingly obey God's will. For since they dwell in perpetual dread as they remain under the sway of the law, they will never be disposed with eagerness to obey God readily unless they have already been given this sort of freedom. . . .

The third part of Christian freedom lies in this: regarding outward things that are of themselves 'indifferent', we are not bound before God by any religious obligation preventing us from sometimes using them and at other times not doing so, as it suits us. And the knowledge of this freedom is very necessary to us, for, if it is lacking, our consciences will have no rest and there will be no end of superstitions. Today we seem to many people to be unreasonable because we stir up discussion upon the unrestricted eating of meat, use of holidays and of vestments, and such things which seem to them vain frivolities. But these matters are more important than is commonly believed. For when consciences once ensnare themselves, they enter a long and inextricable tangle, not easily unravelled. If a man begins to doubt whether he may use linen for sheets, shirts, handkerchiefs, and napkins, he will then be uncertain also about hemp; finally he will even have his doubts about sackcloth. For he will turn over in his mind whether he can eat without napkins, or go without a handkerchief.

To sum up, we see how this freedom works out; namely that we should use God's gifts for the purpose for which he gave them to us, without scruples of conscience or trouble of mind. With such confidence our minds will be at peace with him, and we will recognize his liberality towards us. . . .

Now, since believers' consciences, having received the privilege of their freedom . . . have, by Christ's gifts, attained it, they should not be entangled by any snares of observances in those matters in which the Lord has told them they are free. So we conclude that they are released from the power of all men. For Christ does not deserve to forfeit our gratitude for his great generosity – nor consciences, their profit. And we should not put a low price upon something that we see cost Christ so dearly, since he valued it not with gold or silver but with his own blood. Paul does not hesitate to say that Christ's death is nullified if we put our souls under men's subjection. For, in certain chapters of the letter to the Galatians (Galatians 2, 21) Paul tries to show us how Christ is obscured, or rather extinguished, unless our consciences stand firm in their freedom. That freedom is surely lost if it can be ensnared at man's whim by the bonds of laws and constitutions. But as this is something which is vital to understand, it needs a longer and clearer explanation. For immediately any one breathes a word concerning the overthrow of human laws, huge disputes are stirred up, partly by the seditious, and partly by the slanderers – as if all human obedience were at the same time removed and cast down.

Therefore, in order that no one can stumble upon that stone, let us first consider that there is a twofold government in man: one aspect is spiritual, whereby the conscience is instructed in piety and in reverence towards God; the second is political, whereby man is educated for the duties of humanity and citizenship that must be maintained among men. These are usually called the 'spiritual' and the 'temporal' jurisdiction (not improper terms) by which is meant that the former sort of government applies to the life of the soul, while the latter has to do with the concerns of the present life – not only with food and clothing but with laying down laws whereby man may live his life among other men holily, honourably and decently. For the former lives in the inner mind, while the latter regulates only outward behaviour. The one we may call the spiritual kingdom, the other, the political kingdom. Now these two, as we have divided them, must always be examined separately and while the one is being considered, we must turn aside from thinking about the other. There are in men, so to speak, two worlds, over which different kings and different laws have an authority.

Through this distinction it comes about that we are not to misapply to the political order the gospel teaching upon spiritual freedom, as if Christians were less subject, as concerns outward government, to human laws because their consciences have been set free in God's sight; as if they were released from all bodily servitude because they are free according to the spirit.

Institutes III, xix, 1–15

77   Godly magistrates

The Lord has not only testified that the office of magistrate is approved by and acceptable to him, but he also sets out its dignity with the most honourable titles and marvellously commends it to us. To mention a few scriptural instances; since those who serve us as magistrates are called 'gods' (Exodus 22, 8; Psalms 82, 1), no one should dismiss the fact as being of little importance. For it signifies that they have a mandate from God, having been invested with divine authority, and are wholly God's representatives acting as what might be called his vice-regents. This is no subtlety of mine, but Christ's explanation. 'If scripture', he says, 'called them gods to whom the word of God came . . .' (John 10, 35). . . . Accordingly there should be no doubt that civil authority is a calling, not only holy and lawful before God, but also the most sacred and by far the most honourable of all callings in the whole life of mortal men. . . .

This consideration ought continually to occupy the magistrates themselves, since it can greatly spur them to exercise their office and bring them notable comfort to mitigate the difficulties of their tasks, which are indeed many and burdensome. For what great zeal for uprightness, prudence, gentleness, self-control and innocence ought to be required of those who know that their judgement seat is like the throne of the living God? . . . To sum up, if they remember that they are vicars of God, they should watch with great care, earnestness and diligence, to present to men through themselves some image of divine providence, protection, goodness, benevolence and justice.

Institutes IV, xx, 4 and 6

78 Necessity for civil authority

How foolish is the conceit of those who seek to take away the use of the sword [temporal authority] on account of the gospel. The Anabaptists, we know, have been turbulent, as though all civil order were inconsistent with the kingdom of Christ, as though the kingdom of Christ was made up of doctrine alone, and as though that doctrine was without any influence. We might indeed manage without the sword, were we angels in this world. But the number of the godly, as I have said, is small. It is therefore necessary that the rest of the people should be restrained by a strong bridle; for the children of God are found mixed together, either with cruel monsters or with wolves and rapacious men. Some are indeed openly rebellious, others are hypocrites. The use of the sword will therefore continue until the end of the world.

Minor Prophets (Micah) III, pp. 265–6

79 Tyranny better than anarchy

It is better to live under the most cruel tyrant than without any government at all. Let us suppose all to be on one equal level, what would such anarchy bring forth? No one could wish to yield to others; every one would try the extent of his powers, and thus all would end in prey and plunder, and in the mere licence of fraud and murder, and all the passions of mankind would have full and unbridled sway. Hence I have said that tyranny is better than anarchy, and more easily borne, because there is no supreme governor and there is none to preside and keep the rest in check. . . . God principally wished to show, by this figure, with what intention and with what political order he desires the world to be governed; and why he sets over it kings and monarchies and other magistrates. Then he desired to show, secondly, that although tyrants and other princes forget their duty it is still divinely enjoined upon them and God's grace always shines forth in all governments.

Daniel, pp. 256–7

80   The best form of rule

Obviously it is idle for men in private life, who are disqualified from deliberating upon the organization of any commonwealth, to dispute over what would be the best kind of government in the place where they live. In addition, this question is not simple and requires deliberation since the nature of the solution depends largely upon circumstances. If you compare the forms of government among themselves in isolation from the circumstances, it is not easy to distinguish which one of them excels in usefulness, for they contend upon such equal terms. The fall from kingdom to tyranny is easy; but it is almost as easy to fall from the rule of the best men to the faction of a few; yet it is easiest of all to decline from popular rule to sedition. If the three forms of government which the philosophers discuss are considered in isolation, I will not deny that aristocracy, or a system compounded of aristocracy and democracy, far excels all the others: not indeed in itself, but because it is very rare for kings so to control their will that it never is at variance with what is just and right; or for them to have been endowed with sufficient prudence and shrewdness to know how much is enough. Therefore man's weakness causes it to be safer for a number of men to exercise government so that each one can help, teach and admonish the other. If one of them asserts himself unfairly, there are a number of censors and masters to restrain him.

Institutes IV, xx, 8

81 Obedience to just and unjust magistrates

Let no one be deceived here. Since the magistrate cannot be resisted without God being resisted at the same time, even though it seems that an unarmed magistrate can be despised with impunity, still God is armed to avenge mightily this contempt towards himself. Moreover, under this obedience, I include the restraint which private citizens ought to bid themselves keep in public, that they do not deliberately intrude in public affairs, or needlessly interfere in the office of a magistrate, or undertake anything which is political. If anything in a public law requires amendment, they should not raise a tumult about it, or try to undertake it themselves, but should hand the matter over to the judgement of the magistrates. . . .

We are not only subject to the authority of princes who perform their tasks towards us uprightly and faithfully as they ought, but also to the authority of all those who, by whatever means, have control of affairs, even though they perform only a minimum of the prince's office. For despite the Lord's testimony that the office of a magistrate is the highest gift of his beneficence to preserve the safety of men and, despite his appointment of limits to the magistrates, he still declares at the same time that, whoever they may be, they derive their authority solely from him. Indeed, he says that those who rule for the public benefit are true patterns and evidence of his beneficence; and those who rule unjustly and incompetently have been raised up by him to punish the wickedness of the people; that all equally have been endowed with that holy majesty with which he has invested lawful authority.

Institutes IV, xx, 23–5

82 Magistrates and the protection of subjects' liberties

However these deeds of men are judged, still the Lord accomplishes his work through them alike when he breaks the bloody sceptres of arrogant kings and when he overthrows tyrannical governments. Let princes hear and be afraid.

But we must, in the meantime, be very careful not to despise or violate that authority of magistrates, full of venerable majesty, which God has established by the weightiest decrees, even though it may reside with the most unworthy men, who defile it as much as they can through their own wickedness. For if the correction of unbridled

despotism is the Lord's to avenge, let us not at once think that he has
entrusted it to us, to whom no command has been given except to obey
and suffer.

I am speaking here of private individuals. If there are any magistrates appointed by the people to moderate the power of kings – as in
ancient times the ephors were set against the Spartan kings, or the
tribunes of the people against the Roman consuls, or the demarchs
amongst the senate of the Athenians; and perhaps, as things now are,
such power as the three estates exercise in every realm where they hold
their chief assemblies – I am so far from forbidding them to withstand,
in accordance with their duty, the violence and cruelty of kings, that, if
they connive with kings in their oppression of their people, then I
declare they are guilty of the most wicked perfidy, because they
dishonestly betray the freedom of the people, of which they know that
they have been appointed protectors by God's law.

Institutes IV, xx, 31

B Calvin's Church

Calvin's Church was both an ideal and an institution, both of which
were inspired by God and necessary for salvation. His ideal Church
was the hidden community of saints, the elect, chosen by God, whom
He alone could identify. The ideal was never realizable in full by any
institution on earth, but where the Word of God was properly preached
and the sacraments properly administered then the Church had
something of the doctrine and spirit of the true invisible Church
about it.

The visible Church was vital for the right ordering of evangelical
religion. Calvin was especially eager to defend it against what he saw as
Anabaptist anarchists. In the *Institutes* almost a complete book is
devoted to the visible Church. In many details, Calvin's conception of
the visible Church was identical to that which Luther had established in
the Augsburg confession in 1530.[1] Its chief distinguishing feature lay in
the procedures for self-examination which Calvin envisaged as necessary to keep the visible Church as close to the ideal of the invisible
Church and as free from earthly corruption as possible. It was the same

---

[1] Rupp and Drewery, *Martin Luther*, pp. 144–8.

procedure of mutual criticism which Calvin approved of in mixed government (*see above* p. 62). The first edition of the *Institutes* had little to say on the subject and it was only in the 1543 edition that he described the process of private admonition and public excommunication which he envisaged as both scripturally valid and institutionally practicable in any Church. His views reflected his experience of the Church in Strasbourg and the opinions of Martin Bucer there. Thereafter, Calvin never retreated from his belief that the power to refuse to administer the Lord's Supper was the inalienable power of the visible Church and vital to the preservation of its purity.

83   God's institution of the Church

In our ignorance and laziness we need outward assistance to establish and increase our faith and advance it to its goal, and God has added assistance for our weakness. In order that the preaching of the gospel might flourish, he deposited this treasure in the Church. He instituted pastors and teachers (Ephesians 4, 11) through whose lips he might teach his own. He furnished them with authority; finally he omitted nothing that might make for a holy agreement of faith and right order. He instituted sacraments, which we who have experienced them find to be highly useful aids to foster and strengthen faith. Shut up as we are in the prison house of our flesh, we have not yet attained angelic rank. God, therefore, in his wonderful providence accommodating himself to our capacity, has prescribed a way for us, though still far off, to draw near to him.

Institutes IV, x, 1

84   Visible and invisible Church

We have said that Holy scripture speaks of the Church in two ways. Sometimes by the term 'Church' it means that which is actually in God's presence, into which no persons are received but those who are children of God by grace or adoption and true members of Christ by sanctification of the Holy Spirit. Then, indeed, the Church includes not only the saints presently living on earth, but all the elect from the beginning of the world. Often, however, the name 'Church' designates the whole multitude of men spread over the earth who profess to worship one God and Christ. By baptism we are initiated

into faith in him; by partaking in the Lord's Supper we attest our unity
in true doctrine and love; in the Word of the Lord we can agree, and for
the preaching of the Word the ministry instituted by Christ is
preserved. In this Church are mingled many hypocrites who have
nothing of Christ but the name and outward appearance. There are
many ambitious, greedy, envious persons, evil speakers, and some of
quite unclean life. Such are tolerated for the time being, either because
they cannot be convicted by a competent tribunal or because a
vigorous discipline does not always flourish as it ought.

Just as we must believe, therefore, that the former Church, invisible
to us, is visible to the eyes of God alone, so we are commanded to revere
and keep communion with the latter, which is called 'Church' in a
human context.

Institutes IV, i, 8–9

Accordingly, the Lord has pointed out to us what we should know
about the Church by certain marks and tokens. . . . Wherever we see
the Word of God purely preached and heard and the sacraments
administered according to Christ's institution, there without doubt a
Church of God exists. For his promise cannot fail: 'Wherever two or
three are gathered in my name, there I am in the midst of them'
(Matthew 8, 20).

Institutes IV, i, 8

85–6   Necessity of the Church

Although God's power is not limited to the preaching of the Word, He
has nevertheless commanded us to follow this as our ordinary method
of teaching. Fanatics refuse to hold fast to this, entangling themselves
in many deadly snares. Many are led either by pride, disdain, or
rivalry to the conviction that they can profit enough from private
reading and meditation; hence they despise public assemblies and
deem preaching superfluous. But since they do their utmost to sever or
break the sacred bond of unity, not one of them shall escape the just
penalty of this unholy separation without bewitching himself with
pestilent errors and the foulest delusions.

Institutes IV, i, 5

86

It is not sufficient for one to be thankful to God, for public thanksgiving is also required, so that we may mutually stimulate one another. We also know that confession ought not to be separated from faith; as faith has its seat in the heart, so also outward confession proceeds from it; and therefore it cannot be but that the interior feeling must break out from the soul, and the tongue be connected with the heart. It thus follows that all those who say they have faith within are guilty if they remain silent about it and, as far as they can, try to bury the benefits God has granted them. As I have said, this zeal is required of all the godly, in order that they may stimulate one another to praise God; for it was for this purpose and for this reason that express mention is made of the Temple; that is, that the faithful might understand that God is to be worshipped, not only in private and within closed doors, but that also a public confession ought to be made, so that they may together with common consent celebrate and acknowledge his benefits and blessings.

Jeremiah IV, p. 244

87 Church discipline

Because some people, in their hatred of discipline, recoil even from the word's use, let them understand this: if no society, indeed no house which has even a small family, can be kept in proper condition without discipline, it is much more necessary in the Church, whose condition should be as ordered as possible. Accordingly, as the saving doctrine of Christ is the soul of the Church, so does discipline serve as its sinews, through which the members of the body hold together, each in its own place. Therefore, all who desire to remove discipline or to hinder its restoration – whether they do this deliberately or out of ignorance – are surely contributing to its ultimate dissolution. For what will happen if each is allowed to do as he pleases? The collapse of the Church would surely follow unless the preaching of doctrine was supported by private admonitions, corrections, and other aids of the sort that sustain doctrine and do not let it remain idle.

Institutes IV, xii, 1

88–9   Excommunication and public correction

The case should not come before the Church until the sinner becomes
obstinate. When it does, then the . . . division between crimes and
faults is to be observed. For such great severity is not to be used in
lighter sins, but verbal chastising will be enough – and that mild and
fatherly – which should not harden or confuse the sinner, but bring
him back to himself, that he may rejoice rather than be sad at being
corrected. But shameful acts need to be chastised with a harsher
remedy. Nor is it enough if he, who by setting a bad example through
his offence has gravely injured the Church, be chastised only· with
words; he ought for a time to be deprived of the communion of the
Supper until he gives assurance of his repentance. For Paul not only
rebuked the Corinthian in words, but also banished him from the
Church and reproved the other Corinthians for bearing with him for so
long (I Corinthians 5, 1–7).

Institutes IV, xii, 6

89

The custom of excommunication is ancient and has been exercised in
all ages. Excommunication was . . . a punishment which was used in
ancient times against apostates and despisers of the Law and was used
against Christ's disciples. . . . God determined from the beginning
that there should be some form of correction to restrain rebels. The
priests and scribes not only misused this power tyrannically to harass
the innocent, but at last attacked impiously God himself and his
doctrine. Christ's truth was so powerful that they could not resist it
with laws and regulations so they therefore brandished the thunders of
excommunication to crush it.

The same thing has been done to Christian people. It is impossible to
express the barbarous tyranny which the pseudo-bishops have exercised in subduing the people, so that none dare whisper. And now we
see how cruelly they turn their weapon of excommunication against all
who worship God. But we ought to hold that when excommunication is
applied to a different end by men's passions, it can safely be treated
with contempt. For when God committed to his Church the right to
excommunicate, he was not arming tyrants with a sword or providing
them with executioners to murder poor souls, but was laying down a

rule for governing his people, and that, moreover, on condition that he should hold supreme rule and have men for his ministers. Let the pseudo-bishops thunder as they like. They will not terrify any one with their empty noises, except for those who wander about in uncertainty and doubt, not yet taught by the voice of the Good Shepherd to find the true fold.

In short, nothing is more certain than that those whom we see insubordinate to Christ are deprived of the lawful power of excommunicating. Nor should we fear to be shut out of their assembly, from which Christ, our life and salvation, is also banished. We have no reason at all to dread being thrown out. On the contrary, if we want to be united to Christ, we must withdraw from the synagogues of the Pope of our own accord. Yet although the ordinance of excommunication was so wickedly corrupted in the ancient Church, Christ did not mean it to be abolished by his coming, but restored it to purity, so that it might soundly flourish among us. Although a filthy profanation of this holy discipline prevails in the papacy today, we should, instead of abolishing it, rather use the utmost diligence to restore it to its former integrity. Things will never be so well-ordered in the world but that even the holiest laws of God will degenerate into corruption through men's vice. It would certainly give too much power to Satan, could he annihilate everything he corrupts. We should then have no baptism, no Lord's Supper and, in short, no religion; for he has left no part of it untouched by his pollutions.

St John I, pp. 248–9

90   To the minister at Nördlingen (27 August 1554)

I have never thought that it was a good idea to entrust the right of excommunication to pastors alone. For that would be invidious, of doubtful example, apt to lapse into a tyranny, and the apostles have given us an alternative practice.

CR XLIII, col. 215

C Geneva's *Ecclesiastical Ordinances* (1541)

On Calvin's return, the Genevan magistrates accepted his request that he submit a proper constitution for the reformed Church in the city (*see above* p. 56). The result was the famous *Ecclesiastical Ordinances*, presented to them in September and passed unanimously by them on 20 November 1541. They are of immense importance for they were to be the model followed later everywhere in Europe by the Calvinist Church. They created in Geneva the basis for a self-regulating, visible community of believers whose minister was appointed by laymen to scrutinize and admonish their clergy and whose clergy exhorted and led their flock. Ecclesiastical posts were open to everyone to apply for selection. All was to be conducted with due process of law, order and decorum. The arrangements are a reflection of Calvin's lawyer's skills at drafting constitutions and also of his preference for mixed government.

At the heart of the *Ordinances* lay the institution of the consistory, the regulating body of laity and clergy which would oversee the morals and well-being of the community. Consistories had been attempted (not always with success) in other cities in Reformation Europe by 1541, but Calvin was to establish Geneva's with a vigorous defence of its independence from secular control conducted over the following 15 years. In his initial proposals he had not felt the need to outline any strict divisions of power between civil and ecclesiastical authority. As he later explained (in a passage inserted in the *Institutes* in the 1543 edition), whilst recognizing that there was a difference in kind between ecclesiastical and civil authority, in practice he saw them collaborating, godly saints and godly magistrates, together building a new Jerusalem amidst a worldly Babylon. When the Genevan magistrates saw his draft of the *Ecclesiastical Ordinances* they reacted differently. At every point they modified them (these modifications being indicated in the extracts by the passages italicized and in brackets). The pastors became the paid servants of the Genevan state to whom they owed allegiance. The new elders of the Genevan Church had their appointments ratified by the Genevan council. Thus, neither the proposed consistory court, nor the company of pastors, would have any authority to challenge the supremacy of the Genevan Seignory. In practice, therefore, as Calvin sought to build his new Jerusalem, there would be a generation of bitter disputes over the nature of consistorial and pastoral authority in Geneva.

91   *Ecclesiastical Ordinances* (1541)

First there are four orders of offices instituted by our Saviour for the government of his Church: namely, the pastors, then the doctors, next the elders [*nominated and appointed by the government,*] and fourthly the deacons. If we wish to see the Church well-ordered and maintained we ought to observe this form of government.

The duty of pastors

Pastors are sometimes named in the Bible as overseers, elders and ministers. Their work is to proclaim the Word of God, to teach, admonish, exhort and reprove publicly and privately, to administer the sacraments and, with the elders or their deputies, to issue fraternal warnings.

The examination of pastors

This consists of two parts. The first concerns doctrine – to find out if the candidate has a good and sound knowledge of the Bible; and, secondly, comes his suitability for expounding this to the people for their edification.

Further, to avoid any danger of his having any wrong ideas, it is fitting that he should profess to accept and uphold the teaching approved by the Church.

Questions must be asked to find out if he is a good teacher and he must privately set forth the teaching of our Lord.

Next, it must be ascertained that he is a man of good principles without any known faults.

The selection of pastors

First the ministers should choose someone suitable for the position [*and notify the government*]. Then he is to be presented to the council. If he is approved, he will be accepted and received by the council [*as it thinks fit*]. He is then given a certificate to be produced when he preaches to the people, so that he can be received by the common consent of the faithful. If he is found to be unsuitable and this is demonstrated by evidence, there must be a new selection to find another.

As to the manner of introducing him, because the ceremonies previously used led to a great deal of superstition, all that is needed is that a minister should explain the nature of the position to which he has been

appointed and then prayers and pleas should be made that our Lord
will give him grace to do what is needed.

After election he must take an oath of allegiance to the government
following a written form as required of a minister.

Weekly meetings to be arranged

In the first place it is desirable that all ministers should meet together
once a week. This is to maintain purity and agreement in their teaching
and to hold Bible discussions. Attendance shall be compulsory unless
there is good reason for absence. . . . As for the preachers in the
villages under the control of the government, it is for the city ministers
to urge them to attend whenever possible. . . .

What should be done in cases of difference about doctrine

If any differences of opinion concerning doctrine should arise, the
ministers should gather together and discuss the matter. If necessary,
they should call in the elders and commissioners [*appointed by the
government*] to assist in the settlement of any difficulties.

There must be some means available to discipline ministers . . . to
prevent scandalous living. In this way, respect for the ministry can be
maintained and the Word of God not debased by any minister bringing
it into scorn and derision. Those who deserve it must be corrected, but
at the same time care must be taken to deal with gossip and malicious
rumours which can bring harm to innocent parties.

But it is of first importance to notice that certain crimes are quite
incompatible with the ministry and cannot be dealt with by fraternal
rebuke. Namely heresy, schism, rebellion against Church discipline,
open blasphemy deserving civil punishment, simony and corrupt
inducement, intriguing to take over one another's position, leaving the
Church without special permission, forgery.

There follows the second order which we have called the doctors

The special duty of the doctors is to instruct the faithful in sound
doctrine so that the purity of the gospel is not corrupted by ignorance or
wrong opinion.

As thing stand at present, every agent assisting in the upholding of
God's teaching is included so that the Church is not in difficulties from
a lack of pastors and ministers. This is in common parlance the order of
school teachers. The degree nearest the minister and closely joined to
the government of the Church is the lecturer in theology.

Establishment of a college
Because it is only possible to profit from such teaching if one is first
instructed in languages and humanities, and also because it is necessary to lay the foundations for the future . . . a college should be instituted for instructing children to prepare them for the ministry as well as
for civil government.

In the first place suitable accommodation needs to be provided for
the teaching of children and others who want to take advantage of it.
We also need a literate, scholarly and trained teacher who can take care
of the establishment and their education. He should be chosen and paid
on the understanding that he should have under his charge teachers in
languages and logic, if they can be found. He should also have some
student teachers (*bacheliers*) to teach the little ones. . . .

All who are engaged must be subject to the same ecclesiastical ordinances as apply to the ministers.

There is to be no other school in the city for small children, although
the girls are to have a separate school of their own as has been the case
up to now.

No one is to be appointed without the approval of the
ministers – essential to avoid trouble. [*The candidate must first have been
notified to the government and then presented to the council. Two members of the
'council of 24' should be present at all interviews.*]

Here follows the third order, or elders
Their duty is to supervise every person's conduct. In friendly fashion
they should warn backsliders and those of disorderly life. After that,
where necessary, they should report to the Company [of pastors] who
will arrange for fraternal correction. . . .

As our Church is now arranged, it would be most suitable to have
two elected from the 'council of 24', four from the 'council of 60' and
six from the 'council of 200'. They should be men of good repute and
conduct. . . . They should be chosen from each quarter of the city so
that they can keep an eye on the whole of it.

Method of choosing the elders
Further we have decided upon the machinery for choosing them. The
'council of 24' will be asked to nominate the most suitable and
adequate men they can discover. In order to do this, they should
discuss the matter with the ministers and then present their suggestions
to the 'council of 200' for approval. If they are found worthy [and

approved], they must take an oath in the same form as it is presented to
the ministers. At the end of the year and after the elections to the
council, they should present themselves to the government so that a
decision can be made as to whether they shall be re-appointed or not,
but they should not be changed frequently and without good cause
provided that they are doing their work faithfully.

The fourth order of ecclesiastical government, namely, the deacons
There have always been two kinds of these in the early Church. One
has to receive, distribute and care for the goods of the poor (i.e. daily
alms as well as possessions, rents and pensions); the other has to tend
and look after the sick and administer the allowances to the poor as is
customary. [*In order to avoid confusion*], since we have officials and
hospital staff, [*one of the four officials of the said hospital should be responsible
for the whole of its property and revenues and he should have an adequate salary in
order to do his work properly*].

Concerning the hospital[2]
Care should be taken to see that the general hospital is properly
maintained. This applies to the sick, to old people no longer able to
work, to widows, orphans, children and other poor people. These are
to be kept apart and separate from others and to form their own
community.

Care for the poor who are scattered throughout the city shall be the
responsibility of the officials. In addition to the hospital for those visit-
ing the city, which is to be kept up, separate arrangements are to be
made for those who need special treatment. To this end a room must be
set apart to act as a reception room for those that are sent there by the
officials. . . .

Further, both for the poor people in the hospital and for those in the
city who have no means, there must be a good physician and surgeon
provided at the city's expense. . . .

As for the plague hospital, it must be kept entirely separate.

Begging
In order to stop begging, which is contrary to good order, the

[2] The Geneva general hospital had been established in 1535 in one of the series of
measures by which the city had broken all connections with the Roman Catholic
Church, and which consolidated the various confraternities and eight charitable foundations of the city.

government should use some of its officers to remove any beggars who are obstinately present when people come out of Church.

And this especially if it should happen that the city is visited by this sourge of God.

Of the sacraments
Baptism is to take place only at sermon time and is to be administered only by ministers or their assistants. A register is to be kept of the names of the children and of their parents: the justice department is to be informed of any bastard.

Since the Supper was instituted by our Lord to be more often observed by us and also since this was the case in the early Church until such time as the devil upset everything by setting up the mass in its place, the defect ought to be remedied by celebrating it a little more frequently. All the same, for the time being we have agreed and ordained that it should be administered four times a year, i.e. at Christmas, Easter, Pentecost and the first Sunday in September in the autumn.

The ministers shall distribute the bread in orderly and reverent fashion and no other person shall offer the chalice except those appointed (or the deacons) along with the ministers and for this reason there is no need for many plates and cups.

The tables should be set up close to the pulpit so that the mystery can be more suitably set forth near by.

Celebration should take place only in church and at the most suitable time.

Of the order which must be observed in obedience to those in authority, for the maintenance of supervision in the Church
A day should be fixed for the consistory. The elders should meet once a week with the ministers, on a Thursday, to ensure that there is no disorder in the Church and to discuss together any necessary remedial action.

Since they have neither the power nor the authority to use force, we have agreed to assign one of our officials to them to summon those whom they wish to admonish.

If any one should deliberately refuse to appear, the council is to be informed so as to take action.

If any one teaches things contrary to the received doctrine he shall be summoned to a conference. If he listens to reason, let him be sent back without any scandal or disgrace. If he is obstinate, he should be admonished several times until it is apparent that greater severity is needed: then he shall be forbidden to attend the communion of the Supper and he shall be reported to the magistrates.

If any one fails to come to church to such a degree that there is real dislike for the community of believers manifested, or if any one shows that he cares nothing for ecclesiastical order, let him be admonished, and if he is tractable let him be amicably sent back. If however he goes from bad to worse, after having been warned three times, let him be cut off from the Church and be denounced to the magistrate. . . .

[*All this must be done in such a way that the ministers have no civil jurisdiction nor use anything but the spiritual sword of the word of God as St Paul commands them; nor is the authority of the consistory to diminish in any way that of the magistrate or ordinary justice. The civil power must remain unimpaired. In cases where, in future, there may be a need to impose punishments or constrain individuals, then the ministers and the consistory, having heard the case and used such admonitions and exhortations as are appropriate, should report the whole matter to the council which, in turn, will judge and sentence according to the needs of the case.*]

Registres I, pp. 1–13

92   Formula for excommunication

This was the general formula. Specific names of offenders were introduced at the appropriate point where required.

We have heard, brethren, how our Lord makes his Supper among his disciples, and thereby shows us that strangers – in other words, those who are not of the company of the faithful – ought not to be admitted. Wherefore, in accordance with this rule, in the name and by the authority of the Lord Jesus Christ, I excommunicate all idolaters, blasphemers, despisers of God, heretics, and all who form sects apart to break the unity of the Church, all perjurers, all who are rebellious to parents and to their superiors, all who are seditious, mutinous, quarrelsome, injurious, all adulterers, fornicators, thieves, misers, ravishers of women, drunkards, gluttons, and all who lead a scandalous life; declaring to them that they must abstain from this holy table, for fear of polluting and contaminating the sacred food which our Lord Jesus Christ gives only to his household and believers.

Tracts II, p. 120

V   Enforcement and Opposition

A New Laws and Methods of Enforcement

The consistory provided a potentially powerful means to change the morality of a city and, indeed, a generation; but it required firm laws and a guiding hand from Calvin to prevent petty and narrow-minded attitudes. Laws on marriage, divorce, dancing, promiscuity, blasphemy, drunken behaviour, civic festivals and theatrical performances ensured that the Genevan reformation had a profound effect on the popular culture of the city. Of course in many cases the laws merely restated with greater force earlier civic legislation. But they were rendered effective by the consistory and by regular household visitations undertaken by elders and deacons annually from 1551. Outside the city walls in the 30 villages under Genevan jurisdiction, the consistory's influence was weaker. Here the company of pastors instituted a regular system of visits to each parish to ensure conformity to Genevan regulations. The careful concern of the consistory and ministers in attending to individual cases is notable, even if their ultimate achievement was neither as uniform nor as effective as they would have wished.

93   Ordinances on marriage and divorce

Calvin knew that Geneva's matrimonial legislation would need reforming from its canon law basis to represent Protestant views on marriage. This he regarded as a matter of great importance. He produced a draft of ordinances on the subject for the Genevan council's consideration in 1545. It reflects Calvin's sane and (for the century) liberal views of the position of women in the choice of a spouse and their rights of divorce. The age of majority included in the proposed legislation was substantially lower than that to be found in Calvin's native France. The consistory was to play an important part as a court of reconciliation in marriage questions as well as a court of judgement of sexual offences (*paillardises*). The proposed ordinances were not apparently accepted by the Genevan council although it seems that the consistory took them as its guidelines until they were finally adopted as civil laws in November 1561.

Those who are not allowed to marry without permission

1. Young people, who have not previously been married and whose fathers are alive, cannot contract a marriage unless they have reached the legitimate age, *viz.* 24 years for a young man and 20 years for a young woman. If, after this age, they ask for their fathers' permission and it is refused, then they can marry without consent. . . .

3. If two young people become engaged to be married without consent – through foolishness or lightheadedness – they are to be punished and reprimanded and the marriage is to be rescinded by those who are in charge of them.

4. If any one is found to have been forced to become betrothed, then those responsible shall spend three days on bread and water and afterwards supplicate the magistrates for clemency. . . .

6. There shall be no secret promises between young people who are not yet married, except before two witnesses.

7. If children marry without permission of their father and mother, but at the permitted age, they shall be accepted as having been married because of the over-rigorous attitude of their father. In these cases, fathers shall be compelled to provide a dowry or agree to such terms and conditions [as Genevan laws lay down for dowries] as if they had agreed.

8. No father can constrain his child to a marriage which seems good to him but has not the wishes and consent of the child.

9. At the same time, if, having refused one match against paternal wishes, the child should afterwards choose another, which proves less profitable and advantageous, then, because of the previous disobedience and stubbornness, the father should not be required to give the couple anything during his lifetime.

Celebration of matrimony

When the time comes for the marriage service, the parties should arrive at church modestly, without drummers or fiddlers. They should present themselves with the order and decorum becoming to Christians before the church bells ring so that the marriage can be blessed before the sermon. If they are late or negligent, then they should be sent away.

Causes for a divorce
If a husband accuses his wife of adultery and proves it with witnesses of
sufficient reliability and asks for a divorce, it shall be granted to him.
. . . He shall be asked, however, to pardon his wife, but he should not
be further constrained if he has made up his mind.

It used to be the case that the rights of women did not equal those of
men in the matter of divorce. However, the words of the apostle make
it clear that marriage is reciprocal and a mutual obligation so far as
conjugal rights are concerned. Therefore a wife should be no more
subject to her husband than a husband to his wife. If a man is convicted
of adultery and his wife asks to be separated from him it shall be
granted, provided that the partners cannot be mutually reconciled.

All matrimonial cases concerning conjugal matters (apart from the
property rights involved) should go, in the first instance, before the
consistory where, if they can be happily resolved, they will be settled in
the sight of the Lord. If a judgement in law is required, then the parties
should be sent back to the Genevan council with the opinion of the
consistory in the matter, so that it can be finally decided upon.

CR XXXVIII, cols. 33–44

94 Christian names

Calvin's concern to utilize the power of law to enforce the Reformation
extended to detailed matters of people's lives, including, for example, the
regulation of the Christian names to be used in baptism.

Ordinance of the Genevan council, November 1546
Firstly, the council forbids the use of names of patron saints which used
to dominate the region because it is an encouragement to superstition
and a memory of idolatry from which, by God's grace, we are
delivered. Names like Calude, Suaire, Mama and others, as well as the
names of kings, are forbidden because this is an abuse and has encouraged false allegiances.

Also names like Baptiste, Ange, Evangeliste, etc., because these are
names which belong to those whom God has appointed to these
positions.

Also names belonging to God alone or our Lord Jesus Christ *viz*
Dieu le fils, Esprit, Emmanuel, Sauveur, Jésus.

Also absurd and stupid names such as Toussaint, Croix, Dimanche,

Tiphaine, Sépulchre, Noel, Pasques, Pentécoste, as well as Christian, which is a name common to us all.

Double names and those which do not sound harmonious, such as Gonin, Mermet, Sermet, Allemand.

Also knicknames such as Tyvan, Tevette instead of Estienne, Monet instead of Simon.

Registres I, p. 29

95 Swearing

Calvin presented a memorandum to the Genevan council on behalf of the pastors on the subject of oaths and blasphemy on 18 August 1551. Legislation subsequently followed along the lines suggested in it.

Frivolous oaths

The taking of God's name in vain in an oath is to be prevented. Any one responsible should be told by those who hear him to kneel down and kiss the ground. Those who refuse to do so should be put in prison for 24 hours on bread and water.

Blasphemous oaths

No one is to speak irreverently of God's name. Whoever does so should spend a day and a night in prison on bread and water, after which he should ask for God's pardon at the door of the church nearest to the place where he had committed his offence. On his knees, his head bare, and in the presence of a magistrate, he should ask for God's forgiveness and pay a florin fine (60 *sols*), one half of which should go to the hospital and the other half to the charity account. . . .

Speaking spitefully of God

No one is to speak spitefully of God's name on pain of being put in the stocks for three hours and, from there, being led to prison and fed on bread and water until the following Sunday when he shall be led to the door of the church where he shall ask for God's pardon whilst holding a lighted candle. Those guilty of a second offence will be beaten and banished from the city.

Those who renounce God

Any one who renounces God shall be put in the stocks for six hours and

then led through the streets carrying a torch in public penance, and
then beaten and banished for ever. . . .

CR XXXXVIII, cols. 59-62

96 Festivals

Calvin was careful to follow established practices wherever possible and to
tolerate minor abuses where they did not harm the gospel or the Church. He
made it clear that the unpopular changes in festivals undertaken in 1550 had
not been enacted through his persuasion or with his consent. He also followed
the Genevan laws upon usury and even accepted their relaxation (from a permitted 5 per cent to 7 per cent) in 1557, although with a degree of reluctance.

Another change [16 November 1550] was that the celebration of our
Saviour's nativity should be deferred to the Sabbath day following, and
that there should be no other feast days, except one in seven, which we
call the Lord's Day. This gave offence to a very large number of people
so that some even spread a rumour that the Lord's Day would also be
abolished by Calvin. Their objective was to bring odium upon him,
although the fact was that the matter had been discussed before the
people not only in the absence of any request from the consistory, but
even without their knowledge.

CR XLIX, col. 142 (Beza, *Life of Calvin*)

97 Theatre in Geneva

Minutes of the council of 24
24 May 1546 - A request was received from the drama players . . . to
ask permission to play the *Acts of the Apostles* for the edification of the
people. It was decided that the text should be handed on to M. Calvin
to decide whether it was wholesome and for the public's benefit.

15 June 1546 - M. Calvin, on behalf of the pastors, reported on the
drama the *Acts of the Apostles* saying that the pastors found it to be wholesome and godly but that, for numerous reasons, it seemed to them best
to prevent confusion and disorder that M. Abel [a pastor] should follow
the play's production and be permitted to attend it.

Letter from Calvin to Guillaume Farel, 4 July 1546
Our plays narrowly escaped becoming tragedies. . . . As the day

approached Michael [Cop – a pastor], as he had done once before, preached against the actors. But his sermon was so violent that a crowd of people came immediately to me with loud shouts, threats and so forth. Had I not, by a strong effort, restrained some of their fury they would have come to blows. I endeavoured to appease their exasperations in another sermon, for I judged that he had acted imprudently in having, so unpropitiously, chosen such a theme for a sermon. His extravagance was even more embarrassing since I could not approve of what he had said.

CR XI, col. 355 and XXI, cols. 381–3

98   Household visitation in Geneva

In 1550 it was decided that the ministers should, at appointed times of the year, go round all the wards of the city accompanied by an elder and a deacon to instruct the people and examine every individual briefly as to his faith. This they were to do, not only in sermons, which some neglected and others attended without much apparent benefit, but also in each house and every family. It is scarcely credible how great was the improvement which ensued.

CR XLIX, col. 142 (Beza, *Life of Calvin*)

99   Parish visitation in Geneva's villages

Calvin quickly discovered the difficulties of enforcing the religious changes amongst the 'subjects' in the villages under Geneva's jurisdiction. The persistence of Catholic rituals and the ease with which they evaded ordinances led Calvin to propose in January 1546 a regular annual visitation of all parishes by members of the city's council and the company of pastors in Geneva. In December 1546 the pastors drafted a full set of heads of enquiry for these visitations which were subsequently authorized for use by Geneva's magistrates in May 1547. This shows clearly the enormous problems facing the Calvinist reformation in the countryside and the extent of the change in education and behaviour that was demanded of a rural population.

Ordinance of the syndics and council of Geneva, 11 January 1546
In order, firstly, to preserve an acceptable unity of doctrine throughout the churches of Geneva – that is in the town and the parishes dependent upon it – the magistrates should elect two members of their

council and the company of pastors should elect two from their membership to pay a visit once a year to each parish to check that the minister there has not propounded any new doctrine, against the purity of the holy scriptures.

Secondly, this will also serve to check whether the minister preaches well, or whether he preaches so badly that he teaches nothing, that he is obscure, that he preaches about irrelevant issues; whether he is too strict, or is reprehensible in some way or other.

Thirdly, to exhort the people to go more often to hear sermons, to enjoy them and to profit from them so that they can live Christian lives. . . .

CR XXXVIII, cols. 45-6

Authorized heads of enquiry for a parochial visitation, May 1547
On Sermons
1.   Every household to come to church every Sunday save for those left behind to look after the cattle or the children. Fine 3 *sols*.
2.   If a preaching service has been arranged on a weekday then all who are free to attend should do so and at least one person from each household. Fine 3 *sols*.
3.   Those who have domestics or servant girls should bring them too or send them when they can so that they do not remain in complete ignorance. . . .
5.   During the sermon each should listen attentively without causing disturbances or misbehaving.
6.   No one should leave the church before the end of the sermon without good cause. Fine 3 *sols*.

Catechisms
Since each preacher has two parishes, the catechism should take place in each one every fortnight. Those who have children should send them along with the rest of the household which had not attended the sermon.

Penalties
1.   Churchwardens [*gardes*] should warn heads of households of any fault in themselves or their family.
2.   If, after being warned, they continue in default, they should be fined and a third of the proceeds should go to the warden and two thirds to the parish. . . .

Superstitions
1.   Those found with paternosters or images to worship should be sent
before the consistory, and after punishment there handed over to the
Genevan council.
2.   Those who have been on pilgrimage. . . .
3.   Those who observe papal feast or fasting days. . . .
4.   Those who attend mass. . . .
5.   On all these matters the council will decide whether to imprison
them or impose a special fine.

Blasphemy
1.   An oath by the blood of our Lord or other such oaths will merit, on
the first offence, solemn penance. A second offence will lead to a fine of
5 *sols*, and subsequently it will entail an hour in the stocks.
2.   Those who deny God or renounce their baptism will spend nine
days on bread and water and, for second and third offences, will suffer
more rigorous corporal punishment as the Genevan council shall
determine.

Disagreements with the preaching of scripture
1.   Such contradictions of the Word of God shall be sent before the
consistory and then before the Genevan council to receive the necessary punishment.
2.   If it produces a public scandal which needs prompt action, then the
local policeman [*chastellain*] should deal with it.

Drunken Behaviour
1.   People should not encourage each other to drink so much. Fine 3
sols.
2.   The taverns should be closed during the services. Fine for the inn-
keeper and his customers 3 *sols* each.
3.   Those found to be drunk shall pay, for a first offence, 3 *sols* and be
sent before the consistory; subsequently 5 *sols*, and then 10 *sols* and a
period of imprisonment.
4.   No drinking clubs [*royaulmes*] shall be permitted. Fine 10 *sols*.

Singing and dancing
Those found singing lewd, bawdy or scandalous songs or dancing provocative dances shall be imprisoned for 3 days and then sent before the
consistory.

Usury
No one shall lend usuriously, making more than 5 per cent profit on pain of confiscation of the loan and an additional appropriately stiff fine.

Assault
1. Those who pick quarrels shall be punished accordingly.
2. Any one who forms a gang or acts seditiously in the pursuit of a vendetta will be punished more severely as appropriate.

Feuds
If there are any feuds or hatreds amongst individuals, the minister shall call in his churchwardens and attempt to pacify them. If he does not succeed, the parties should be sent before the consistory.

Betting
No one should play depraving games, either for gold or silver or excessive stakes of any kind. Fine 5 *sols* and confiscation of the winnings.

Sexual offences
1. Unmarried couples guilty of a sexual offence will be imprisoned for six days on bread and water and will pay 60 *sols*.
2. Adultery (i.e. if one or the other party is married) will lead to imprisonment for nine days and a fine appropriate to this more serious offence, to be imposed by the magistrates.
3. Those who are engaged to be married should not live together as man and wife until their marriage has been solemnized in church lest they be treated as guilty of a sexual offence.

Registres I, pp. 14–19

B Opposition to Calvin – the Genevan Context

Calvin's religious changes and the vigour with which they were enforced created widespread opposition and a deep-rooted distrust of all the ministers. It began to appear in 1545 and was to last as a serious threat to Calvin's continued stay in Geneva for a decade. In 1545 Geneva was visited by a virulent outbreak of the plague. The Genevan magistrates denied Calvin's request to minister to the plague suspects, isolated in a temporary hospital outside the city walls, lest he become contaminated. But in the immediate aftermath of the outbreak Calvin was accused of having given encouragement to witch doctors who, it was alleged, had malevolently spread the plague about the city. The same rumours had been put about in 1533 when there had been another outbreak of plague and when the reform had just arrived in the city. Since heresy was frequently seen as disease or infection in the body politic, the connection between visitations of the plague and Calvin's work in the city was natural and inevitable. The magistrates dealt with the rumour by arresting and later burning the suspected witches, and Calvin supported these vigorous actions. It is the only recorded instance of Calvin giving any encouragement to witchcraft persecution.

In the following year, 1546, the opposition to Calvin began to coalesce into a loose faction, typical of those factions which had been evident in the city earlier in the century (*see above*, pp. 44–7). Its leader was a young man called Ami Perrin, from a distinguished and wealthy Genevan family which had strongly supported Geneva's independence and assisted in bringing about Calvin's return from Strasbourg in 1541. Like many Genevans, he became suspicious of the influx of refugees into the city, afraid that the Emperor Charles V would take advantage of his war in Germany with the princes to capture Geneva, and increasingly frustrated by the powers of the consistory. He and his wife had a taste for exotic clothes and for dancing parties, and neither displayed much interest in the finer points of dogma. In 1547 he was elected captain-general of the city's militia, an important post of considerable influence within the city walls. The youth militia was regarded by the ministers as a focus for misrule in the city and their flamboyant style of dress became an issue in the summer of 1547 between the Perrin faction and the ministers. Towards the end of the year Perrin was despatched to the court of Henry II of France upon an embassy. On his return he was accused of treason, having offered (it was alleged) to introduce a French garrison into Geneva to secure the city from attack by Charles V's troops in southern Germany. A lengthy trial ensued in which Calvin's supporters came out badly. Perrin was acquitted and restored to his office in the Genevan state from which he was able to play a part in the second wave of opposition to Calvin which gathered strength in 1551.

100 Plague and conspiracy

The following year [1545] began with contests and these were by far the most damaging in which he [Calvin] had so far been involved. For, as if the plague sent from heaven had not sufficiently exhausted the city and its neighbourhood, avarice prevailed to such an extent that some poor wretches, whom the richer classes had employed to take care of the sick and to purify their houses, formed a horrible conspiracy together, and smeared the door-posts and thresholds as well as the passages of houses with a pestilential ointment which immediately produced a dreadful plague. They had agreed with each other under a solemn oath to become the bond-slaves of Satan if they were induced by any torture to betray their accomplices. Several were, however, apprehended, both in the city and around it, and they suffered an appropriately severe punishment. It is almost incredible how much infamy Satan, by this device, brought upon Geneva and especially on Calvin, since people believed that the Devil was obviously reigning in the very place where, in fact, he was being most energetically opposed.

CR XLIX, col. 136 (Beza, *Life of Calvin*)

101–2 The Libertine faction (1546–8)

The state of the city was especially troubled. There were frequent rumours of preparations which the Emperor [Charles V] was said to be making against the [reformed] religion, and of the wiles of the Pope (who was said to have arsonists in his pay).[1] As a result it was necessary to strengthen the morale of the citizens. The perniciousness of the wicked ones, far from being broken by their setbacks so far, continued instead to increase and at length to break out into the open. They obtained as their leader some one called Ami Perrin, an exceedingly foolish but daring and ambitious man whom, for this reason, Calvin used to call in his letters the 'comic Caesar' and who, some time before had succeeded in getting the people to vote him into the office of captain-general. Thinking, as well he might, that he and those like him could have no footing while the laws were in force, and especially whilst Calvin was constantly thundering against their evil, he began at last, in this year, to show what he and his faction were meditating. . . . For, a

[1] Charles V mobilized his troops for the Schmalkaldic War in May 1546; in June 1546 he signed an agreement with Pope Paul III for assistance in the campaigns.

short while afterwards, a reasonably attended meeting of the council
was convened. One of the magistrates (secretly instigated apparently
by two members of the consistory, both of whom were prone to
drunkenness, and neither of whom feared the legal consequences)
openly accused Calvin of preaching false doctrine.

CR XLIX, col. 138

102

8 April 1546 – Register of the consistory
The wife of the sieur Ami Perrin appeared and was accused of having
danced at Belle Rive and at the house of the sieur Antoine Lect. She
denied it, although she admitted that she had seen others dancing and
that she enjoyed dancing herself. She accused the court of victimizing
her father, her brother and her brother-in-law. She was reprimanded
for this accusation. She said that she wished to defend the cause of her
father and added that her father should be investigated in private and
not in public. She was told that they would treat him as they treated any
one in the city. She was again asked to name those who had been dancing and she replied twice that she would prefer to be corrected by the
city magistrates and face civil justice rather than the consistory court.

CR XXI, col. 377 (The minute of the
court record has been expanded into full
sentences.)

Calvin to Guillaume Farel, April 1546
After your departure, the dancing caused us more difficulties than I
had foreseen. . . . Francisca, the wife of Perrin, grossly abused us. . . .
I replied as was appropriate and as she deserved. I enquired whether
their house was so sacred that it owed no subjection to the laws. We
already hold in detention her father, convicted of one act of adultery
with proof of a second near at hand and reports of the third growing
stronger. Her brother has openly slandered the magistrates of the city
and ourselves. Finally, I added that a new city would have to be constructed for them to live on their own unless they would be willing to be
restrained by us here under the yoke of Christ.

CR XL, cols. 334–5

103 Slashed breeches and the youth militia (1547)

Calvin to the faithful brethren of France, 24 July 1547

The condition of our young people is very corrupt so that when we do not let them do exactly as they please they become very difficult to bridle and control. Of late, they have become enraged by an insignificant issue. It was that they were not allowed to wear slashed breeches[2] which have been prohibited for the past 12 years. The matter itself is of no great importance to us but it is clear that the tucks in these breeches would be the breach leading to other disorders. We protested that slashed breeches were merely a matter of fashion and not worth bothering about and that we were concerned with the wider objective of curbing and repressing misrule. During this little dispute the Devil has stirred up others so that there has been a great deal of grumbling. Because they find that we are prepared to stand up to them and show greater resilience and courage than they had anticipated, the venom which some of them had felt for us but kept enveloped in their hearts now burst forth.

CR XL, cols. 561–2

104 Trial of Perrin and reinstatement

At last, Perrin, having by his audacity brought himself into great danger, was as a result expelled from the council, deprived of his office of captain and reduced to the rank of private citizen. But, though all these things were transacted in open council, it is impossible to measure the trouble they gave Calvin himself. Indeed, on one occasion [15 December 1547] in the 'council of 200' the quarrel rose to such a pitch that they were on the point of drawing swords and staining the council chamber itself with blood. During the disturbance Calvin came in with his colleagues and suppressed it (although at risk to his life) even though the factious proceedings of these men were directed particularly at him. He proceeded nevertheless to express his utter detestation of their crimes, and rebuke them with the severity which they deserved. . . .

In 1548 the old faction again burst forth . . . Perrin was restored but, as a result, the malice of the wicked rose to such a height that some

---

[2] i.e. breeches with a distinctive silk dart inserted into the garment worn by the youth militia.

of them openly used collars cut in the form of a cross, for the purpose of mutual recognition, while others gave the name of Calvin to their dogs or, playing on the name, changed Calvin to Cain. Finally, some declared that as a result of their enmity towards him they would not join him in the Lord's Supper. All these proceedings were rebuked sharply by Calvin and his colleagues and the disputing groups were summoned before the Council and . . . ultimately an amnesty was ratified on 18 December by a solemn oath.

CR XLIX, cols. 140–1

105   Climax to Genevan opposition (1551–5)

During this period the issue of the religious refugees who were appearing in the city in increasing numbers, mainly from France (*see below* pp. 122–4), became particularly acrimonious. Eventually, the support of the refugees would be important in Calvin's triumph.

The dissensions of the following year [1551] far outweighed the two previous years of tranquillity, and the wickedness of the factious ones erupted the more furiously the longer it was smothered, to the extent that they openly refused to confer the freedom of the city of Geneva upon the exiles who had settled there.[3] Not content with this alone, they jostled Calvin himself as he returned from preaching on the other side of the Rhône, and they almost drowned his colleague Raymond by secretly removing the props to the bridge which he used to cross the river one night. They even stirred up a large mob at the church of St Gervais because the minister refused to give the name of Balthasar to a child which had been presented for baptism [*see above*, p. 79]. . . .

The following year [1553] was so turbulent, since the malice of the factious ones was reaching its climax, that both Church and republic in Geneva stood in grave danger. Their clamours and menaces reached such heights that, at length, by suppressing the liberties of good people, they secured some changes in the ancient statutes upon the question of the appointment of Genevan magistrates, . . . expelled some from the council and, upon the pretence of a fear of foreign exiles within the city, deprived them of all weapons (except their swords) when they ventured beyond its walls. As a result, it seemed that nothing would prevent them from accomplishing the design for which they had long plotted. . . .

[3] On 6 February 1551 they were excluded from the status of *bourgeois*.

They went to such lengths [in 1554] that they transformed the Word of God into obscene songs and beat any foreigners whom they met in the dark, sometimes even robbing them. . . .

In 1555, by a wonderful blessing from God, the divisions at home were put to one side and Geneva was given its well-deserved peace. The faction ruined itself by its own work, for a dreadful conspiracy was discovered amongst them, thanks to the obstinate audacity of some of the conspirators whilst they were drunk. Some of them were executed and others were exiled, and although the latter continued to trouble the state in Geneva, they eventually met shameful ends, thus affording a singular example of the slow but just punishment from God.

> CR XLIX, cols. 143, 148, 149, 153 (Beza, *Life of Calvin*)

106 Conspiracy of 18 May 1555

On the night of 18 May 1555 the Libertine faction endeavoured to instigate a municipal insurrection against the foreigners in the city. Calvin reported the failure of the riot to Bullinger with quiet satisfaction on 5 June 1555. His account (and a more detailed one two weeks later) exaggerated certain aspects of the plot.

A single night nearly brought ruin to us all and upon the city as well. But by the miraculous counsels of God it has turned out that we have been saved by those who, unknown to us, constituted our greatest threat. When that faction which has been continually hostile to us for the last three years saw themselves thoroughly defeated, they decided upon a move typical of those who are desperate. It is true that slaves were not freed from their chains as they used to be in the past when there were slaves, but worthless vagabonds were gathered together in the taverns and their services bought like mercenaries. Evidence has established beyond question that free banquets were offered in two such places to a band of scoundrels and then, suddenly, a tumultuous attack was made upon the city watch. As there were not a hundred men involved, they began to call, frantically, every one to arms. The French, they repeatedly cried, the French had betrayed the city. Of the French, not a single one appeared. Some citizens followed the syndics who were aroused from their beds. They were exposed to violence such that nothing like it had been witnessed within living memory. The result was, however, very different from what these rioters had anticipated. They had decided that if any of the French showed themselves they would eliminate them, cry victory, and immediately afterwards butcher the four syndics and the leaders of the council. But the Lord exposed them, stripped them of their false pretences, and derided them.

CR XLIII, cols. 640–1

C Three Genevan Opponents of Calvin – Ameaux, Gruet and Troillet

Three examples of those who opposed Calvin – many others could have been chosen – give a clear idea of the hostilities he aroused and how he dealt with them. Pierre Ameaux was a printer of playing cards and a manufacturer of dice, an active politician and city office-holder who had supported Calvin's return in 1541. Fear for his livelihood as well as his matrimonial problems led him to criticize Calvin. Calvin personally indicted Ameaux before the Genevan magistrates, had him imprisoned and declared ineligible for public office, and extracted a humiliating public apology from him in April 1546.

The case of Jacques Gruet was more serious but required less activity on the part of Calvin. He was a prominent and respected Genevan *bourgeois* who objected to the growing domination by Calvin of public affairs. His personal behaviour apparently left something to be desired and he was also suspected of favouring French intervention in Geneva. On 27 June 1547 a notice was placed on the pulpit of the church of St Pierre which criticized the clergy; Gruet was its suspected author and he was arrested. His house was subsequently searched and papers were discovered which proved beyond question that Gruet held the Bible in open contempt. His religious tenets were blasphemous and his political propositions treasonable. They were used against him in the subsequent trial in which he defended himself with vigour and he was executed on 26 July 1547. Calvin took no direct part in the trial although he did advise the magistracy upon Gruet's irreligion.

Jean Troillet (Trolliet) came from an old Genevan family and had attempted to join the ministry in the city. Calvin had rejected him as unsuitable and he subsequently obtained employment as a city notary. He became a supporter of Perrin and criticized Calvin openly, publicly disagreeing with the doctrine of predestination upon the familiar ground that it made God the author of sin. There was a public debate before the council in which Calvin, with the support of Guillaume Farel and Pierre Viret, refuted Troillet's assertions. The council eventually declared in favour of Calvin and its strong support for the reformer forced Troillet to admit defeat. They were publicly reconciled and Troillet retired to obscurity.

Genevan opposition centred both upon the enforcement of the Reformation and upon certain aspects of doctrine. Towards the former, however, most Genevan *bourgeois* appeared to be ambivalent, and upon the latter trained theologians from elsewhere in Europe were more able to articulate their objections. Calvin dealt characteristically with his opponents. He appealed to law, relied upon precedent, cited his vocation, utilized his mastery of Biblical quotations and wielded his powerfully trained logic and advocacy against them. When circumstances demanded it, Calvin could be strongly convincing if also, at first sight, unattractively remorseless. As Troillet remarked, 'He takes no pleasure in being criticized.'

107 Pierre Ameaux

Register of the council of 24, 27 January 1546
It is reported that Ameaux said that M. Calvin was a bad man, a mere Picard, who preached false doctrine. He was prepared to uphold this statement as is more fully indicated by the information received. Ordered: that he shall be imprisoned and an action heard against him later.

Ibid., 8 April 1546
Having perused the contents of his [Ameaux's] replies it appears that he has wickedly spoken against God, the government and M. Calvin and that this is abundantly clear from his answers. Ordered: that he shall be sentenced to walk round the city in his shirt, bare-headed, with a lighted candle in his hand and then beg for mercy on his knees before the Bench, confessing that he has spoken evilly. He is condemned to pay all the costs and the sentence is to be publicly promulgated.

CR XLIX, cols. 368, 377

Calvin to Guillaume Farel, February 1546
Fifteen days ago the card-maker was locked up because while at supper in his house he spoke with such uncontrollable violence and insolence

against me that he must have been out of his mind. I kept quiet about
this except that I informed the judges that it would not be agreeable to
me if they proceeded against him to the utmost limit of the law. I
wanted to visit him. Access was forbidden by the authorities. And yet
some good men charge me with cruelty in being so eager to avenge my
injuries. I have been asked by his friends to accept the offices of an
intermediary. This I have refused to do except on two conditions, that
no suspicion should fall upon me and that Christ's honour should not
be impugned. I am now clear of the matter. I await the verdict of the
council.

CR XL, col. 284

108   Jacques Gruet

Jacques Gruet to the magistrates of Geneva, c. July 1547
It seems to me that a public authority should so arrange its affairs that it
never has to ask its subjects to approve something which would subject
them against their nature and thus cause discord. No king or
republican régime whatsoever allows a subject to do something which
he would not wish done to him – for example that one subject should
murder another. . . .

But if I am the sort who wants to manage my affairs as I please, what
concern is it to any one else? If I want to dance, leap about and have a
good time, what concern is that to the judicial authorities? None whatsoever. Sometimes an overweening judicial power results in many
machinations which allow one man to be the cause of many evils and
the deaths of thousands of men as we see by bitter experience in our
time in France.

CR XL, cols. 564–5

From the records of Gruet's trial
He recognized that he had been ill-advised and seduced into attacking
in his writings authors such as Moses who wrote the law of God by the
inspiration of the Holy Spirit. He had maintained that Moses was a
man just like other men, and in this way he tried to reduce to nothing
the teaching of Moses. This could lead to the great confusion and
scandal of the faithful. He further maintained that all laws, divine and
human alike, were made by men for their own pleasure, together with

other wicked assertions so heinous as not to be put on record. . . .

He had written a notice in his own hand which he had affixed to the pulpit of the church of St Pierre which offended God and threatened His agents and servants with death, a wicked action. His intention had been to overthrow God's holy Word. . . .

After he had been instructed from God's holy teaching and from the Bible both in writing and by ministers so that he knew the difference between good and evil, he had persevered in his wicked course as evidenced by letters in his own handwriting. . . .

All his life, deceived by an evil spirit, he preferred doing evil to doing good . . . so that his villainies and enormities were so great as to defy description.

CR XL, cols. 565–7

Sentence – 26 July 1547
You have outrageously offended and blasphemed against God and his holy Word; you have conspired against the government; you have threatened God's servants and, guilty of treason, merit capital punishment.

CR XL, col. 567

Calvin to Pierre Viret, 2 July 1547
Next day a paper was found in the pulpit threatening us [the ministers] with death unless we kept quiet. The council, startled by such audacity, ordered a strict enquiry to be made into the conspiracy. . . . They immediately arrested Gruet who was widely suspected as its author. The writing was not, in fact, his; but while they looked through his papers they discovered others which were just as incriminating. There was a humble petition which he had intended to present to the 'council of 200' in which he proposed that no offence should be punished by law except when it was injurious to the state. This, he argued, was the practice of the Venetians who were the highest authority in matters of government. Truly, there was a considerable danger that a thousand souls here might have been lost because of the brainchild of one deranged man. Letters were also discovered. . . . In some of them I was named, and in others I was referred to in such a crude allegory that it was easy to see whom he had in mind. There were also two pages of Latin in which the whole of scripture was mocked, Christ ridiculed, the

immortality of the soul called a fairy story and the whole of religion
pulled to pieces. I do not think he was the author of it, but it was in his
handwriting.

109   Jean Troillet

Calvin's reply to Troillet before the Genevan council, 9 October 1552
I certainly agree that I wrote that God not only foresaw but also
ordained the fall of Adam, which I maintain to be true, not without
good reason and proof from Holy Writ. When he accuses me of having
written that by the ordinance and will of God man is obliged to sin, as I
have often said before, I should much prefer that people should not
attribute to me this monastic jargon which I have never used. Only
hypocrites [*caffars*] drone on like this in their barbarous way. Let us
consider the doctrine as I have set it out. I do indeed admit that evil
doers necessarily sin and that this necessity comes of God's ordinance
and will. But I also insist that necessity does not imply obligation; the
sinner cannot say by way of excuse that he was acting under compul-
sion. This doctrine I can prove so completely and thoroughly from the
Bible that no one living can possibly disagree with it. And I maintain
that the other side should not cunningly put the blame on me, and
further that the very evident proofs that I have put in my books should
not be evaded. He says that he has maintained the contrary opinion
without wishing or being able to accept mine. If he were the wisest man
in the world it would still be usurping authority for him to want his
answer to be accepted simply because he neither will nor can agree to
what is suggested to him. Still less is there any reason why a man who
knows very little about the Bible and is not competent to judge upon
matters of theology should expect that at his mere wish those to whom
God has given grace to know rather more should be reproved.

If the proofs, my Lords, that you have heard are not enough for you,
I can offer to expound them more fully whenever and at such length as
you wish. For the rest, I rely upon what is contained in the book on the
predestination and providence of God.[4]

CR XLII, cols. 378–9

---

[4] Calvin had published that year a work on *The Eternal Predestination of God* which summarized his views (*De Aeterna Praedestinatione Dei*, 1552).

Decision of the Genevan council against Troillet, 9 November 1552
After hearing the case for and against Calvin and Troillet, consideration was given to Calvin's *Institutes*. After due consideration, the
council concluded that the matter had received full attention and
declared the said book, the *Institutes*, to have been well and piously
written, that its teaching was that of God's holy doctrine, that he
[Calvin] was a good and true minister in this city and that henceforth
no one should venture to contradict the said book or its doctrine. Both
parties and all concerned were required to accept this decision.

CR XLII, col. 385

D Bolsec, Castellio and Servetus

Three foreigners provided the most serious doctrinal challenge to
Calvin. From their different backgrounds in France, Italy and Spain,
they all gravitated at some time during the period from 1541 to 1553 to
Geneva, attracted partly by its freedom and tolerance. Each took up a
separate but interrelated issue of Calvin's theology and by their efforts
Geneva became a centre for theological controversy during this period,
and emerged from it with a more clearly defined, but more rigid and
narrow orthodoxy.

a) Jérôme Bolsec and the issue of predestination

Jérôme Bolsec (*c*. 1520–84) was an ex-Carmelite monk and a Doctor of
Theology from the university of Paris. He accepted the reform in 1545
and spent some time at the court of Renée of France, just as Calvin had
done (*see above* p. 43). There he married, studied medicine and became
the personal physician to a friend of Calvin. In 1551 Bolsec arrived in
Geneva and accepted Calvinism with zeal, except for the precise
conception of predestination. He presented his objections before the
ministers of the city on 16 October 1551, asserting that Calvin's
theology made God into a tyrant, condemning and saving souls at
pleasure, and also into the author of sin, responsible for good and evil
in the world. He was imprisoned by the magistrates on charges of
offensive language, blasphemy and heresy, and a long interrogation
followed in which Calvin played a leading part. The magistrates
eventually decreed on 22 December 1551 that Bolsec should be

banished from the city. He retired to Berne and returned to France towards the end of his life where he was reconverted to Catholicism and wrote an important but highly prejudiced account of Calvin's life from which much subsequent criticism of the reformer has been drawn.[5]

110   Jérôme Bolsec's propositions

Thirteen propositions were extracted by the pastors from the lecture Bolsec gave to them on 16 October 1551.

1.   He declared that there was a pernicious new opinion, contrary to the Word of God and holy scripture, that before the creation of the world God had predestined those who were to be saved and those who were to be damned before he had foreseen those who would be believers.

4.   Wishing to prove that the reprobate were those who resisted the Word of God, he referred to passages in scripture where God attributed the damnation of men to their own evil and concluded that these texts proved that God did not condemn men because they were reprobate but because they did not believe. Thus, unbelief preceded reprobation.

10.   He condemned the doctrine of God that we follow, saying that it conceived of God as a tyrant and an idol like the Jupiter created by pagans. . . .

11.   He also added that, in saying that God had predestined us to life or death, we make God into the author of evil and iniquity.

12.   Moreover, he said that we provided grounds for the wicked to decry God by saying that they could do nothing about it if they were damned and that it was not their fault.

CR XXXVI, cols. 147–9

111   Calvin's reply

Blosec's further criticisms drew from Calvin a long and detailed refutation of what he saw as maliciously inspired remarks about his theology.

For my part, he [Bolsec] slanders me falsely when he says that I have written that God necessitates men to sin. To begin with, this word 'necessitates' is not part of my vocabulary, but a monkish term that I

---

[5] J. Bolsec, *Histoire de la vie, moeurs, actes, doctrine, constance et mort de Iean Calvin* (G. Chaudière, Paris, 1577).

have never used. It is impudent to say that I should never have used this word 'sin' in the context of the will of God. I have stated, it is true, that the will of God, the supreme cause, is necessary for everything. But I have also maintained, in any case, that God disposes as he wishes, and in all he does shows such strict equity that the most wicked are forced to glorify him, his will not being tyrannous or unreasonable but rather the dominion of complete goodness. . . .

Bolsec finally tries to hide his wicked errors in his own doctrine, as, for example, when he says that God has granted to each one of us, in our hearts, the ability to obey him in faith. This implies that his will does not rule over us but that men can, of their own free will, accept as seems good to them the grace of the Holy Spirit. As a result, our election and salvation depend on our own merits. In fact, he maintains that men have not lost their own free will for, without it, they would be no better than wild beasts.

When Bolsec says that the grace of God is bestowed equally on us all, and that men can themselves choose between salvation and damnation, this is to deny that God has chosen by his own free goodness those whom he will have as his children; and further this is to deny that, after their salvation, God will not guide their affections and hearts to lead them to Jesus Christ; and that, once brought thither, he would not hold them so to the end.

CR XXXVI, cols. 182–3

112   Bolsec's banishment (23 December 1551)

Register of the council of 24
Having heard the case brought and maintained before us by our lieu-tenant against you, Jérôme Bolsec, native of Paris, in which you and your supporters . . . have raised false opinions before the holy company of pastors and sustained them against the holy scriptures and the pure evangelical religion. . . . By this our firm decision we condemn you . . . to be banished in perpetuity and we exclude you from this city and its territories. . . .

CR XXXVI, col. 247

b) Sebastian Castellio and the issue of toleration

Sebastian Castellio (Castellion, Castalio, 1515–63) was a Savoyard
scholar and humanist whom Calvin had first met in Strasbourg. He
had invited him to Geneva in 1541 to run the school (*see above* p. 73). In
1543 Castellio presented himself as a candidate for the ministry but was
found to hold inadmissable views on the Song of Songs as not part of
holy scripture, a matter on which Calvin would allow no discussion.
There were also differences of opinion over the descent of Christ into
hell. Castellio's appeals to reason and common sense were brushed
aside. He was refused a place in the Genevan ministry and he later
withdrew to Lausanne and was eventually appointed professor of
Greek at the university of Basel in 1553. This was still a centre for
humanist toleration, and Castellio produced a series of works against
Calvin's intolerance, beginning with an essay upon predestination in
support of Bolsec, and subsequently publishing (under an assumed
name and with a fraudulent imprint) a compilation powerfully supporting freedom of conscience. This work (*Concerning heretics and whether
they should be punished by the sword of the magistrates*, 1554) was a most
powerful criticism of Calvin's attitudes and actions in the Servetus
affair. It became the most important text for debates over religious
toleration during the next century and a half.

113   Castellio's testimonial

After Castellio was refused a place in the Genevan ministry he asked for a
testimonial from the pastors of the city to obtain the post of school master in
Lausanne. The report was signed by Calvin in February 1544.

When Sebastian Castellio was head of our school he formally applied to
the council for a transfer. For he had taken up this appointment on
condition that he would relinquish it altogether if, after a period of
probation, he was found to be unsuitable. Wanting to change, he asked
us for a testimonial about his earlier career, which we could not refuse.
    We testify briefly that his conduct while with us was such that all
would have agreed to his acceptance as a pastor except for one issue.
For when we enquired as usual as to whether he agreed with us upon
our doctrine, he said there were two matters where he could not. These
were
(a) that we included the Song of Solomon among the books of the Bible
and

(b) that the descent of Christ into hell was explained in the catechism as referring to the intensity of his suffering. . . .

Our chief difference of opinion was about the Song of Songs. He thought that this was simply a lascivious or obscene song describing Solomon's objectionable love affairs. Our first plea and entreaty was that he should not rashly reject the age-long interpretation of the whole of the Church. There was no controversial book about which there had not been at some time or another a measure of uncertainty and dispute. Some, which we now recognize as authoritative, were not originally received without discussion: the Song of Songs was never publicly repudiated. We implored him to be more moderate in his opinions and especially not to differ from every one who had preceeded him. . . . When this reasoning appeared to have no weight with him, we consulted among ourselves about what was to be done next.

First of all, good people would be seriously offended if they heard that we were appointing a minister who publicly rejected and condemned a book which all Churches included in the canon of sacred books. This would be for us to open a window to evil-disposed and ungodly people who would seize on the opportunity for attacking the gospel and dividing the Church. Further, at this rate we should be obliged in the future not to turn away any one else who wanted to eliminate Ecclesiastes or the Proverbs or any other book from the rest: this might even mean that discussions could start as to which book was worthy or unworthy of the Holy Spirit.

CR XXXIX, cols. 673–5

114 Calvin to Sulzer (7 August 1554)

Castellio, believe me, is a creature both malignant, unmanageable and pernicious. Under the masque of charity and even of modesty, he hides the most inconceivable arrogance. He and some others have put together a pamphlet stuffed full of the most atrocious outrages against me with the intention of its causing some sudden attack to be made upon me here [in Geneva].

CR XLIII, col. 209

c) Michael Servetus and the issue of the Trinity

More than any other single episode, the death at the stake of Servetus
has caught the attention of the world. It has been represented as the
triumph of prejudice and force over intelligence and compromise, of
Calvin's narrow-minded fanaticism over Servetus' toleration, of
Calvin's theocracy over common sense. In its origins, the Servetus
affair was part of the age-long discussion of the meaning of the Trinity
which had exercised the thought of the early Church, existed under-
ground throughout the Middle Ages and emerged in the sixteenth
century with the anti-Trinitarianism of Gribaldi, Cellarius, Ochino,
Socinus and Servetus himself.

A Spaniard from the Basque region by birth, Michael Servetus
(1511-53) may have known at an early age the difficulties experienced
by the Arab and Jewish minorities in the Spanish peninsula in understanding the Christian orthodoxy on the Trinity. Servetus studied in
Toulouse, Basel and Paris, where Calvin met him briefly in 1534 whilst
he was using his assumed name of Michel de Villeneuve (*see above* p. 9).
Wherever he went he associated with heterodoxy, and whatever he
published betrayed his radical leanings. His first works of theology
attacked the conventional notions of the Trinity in 1531-2. His
medical and anatomical researches led him to question traditional
medicine and suggest the theory of the circulation of the blood round
the body. For his astrology he was subsequently condemned by the
Sorbonne and forbidden to teach in Paris. His polyglot Bible of
1542 drew systematically and extensively upon Jewish, Gnostic, pan-
theistic, and neo-Platonic traditions of Biblical exegesis and it was
shortly after this work was published that he wrote his main work of
systematic theology entitled The *Restoration of Christianity* (*Christianismi
Restitutio*). In this work Christ was pictured as indeed the Son of God
but as neither co-eternal nor of the same substance with the Father.
The Word [*Logos*] pre-existed with the Father and Christ combined
Word and flesh and was therefore not entirely human. Salvation was
not by faith alone. Original sin was a misconception and infant
baptism was absurd, for mortal sin could not be committed under the
age of 20. Like Calvin only in his belief that Christianity had lost its
primitive purity, Servetus hoped that his book would live up to its title
and restore that purity. In fact, it became the casebook for all unorthodox religious thinkers in the following century.

Some passages of the manuscript of Servetus's book were sent
through a bookseller in Lyons, Jean Frellon, to Calvin for his

comments. Calvin immediately reacted adversely and suspected who had written them. Later, when it was finally published in 1553 with Calvin's comments upon those passages sent to him as a preface, Calvin wrote quickly to the pastors of the Church at Frankfurt to try to prevent its distribution at the Frankfurt book fair. Meanwhile Calvin alerted the Inquisition in Lyons to the existence of Servetus in Vienne. He used a Protestant exile from Lyons, one Guillaume. Trie, as an intermediary for the purpose. Servetus was duly investigated by the Inquisition and imprisoned at Vienne. But, to Calvin's surprise and indignation, he escaped and made his way to Geneva, en route, probably, for Basel. However, he was quickly recognized and imprisoned in August 1553. At the subsequent prosecution for heresy in Geneva Calvin was represented by his secretary, Nicolas de la Fontaine. There was a great deal of argument in the course of the trial, both verbal and written. Servetus presented his case in great detail, with supporting biblical texts and quotations from the pre-Nicene fathers. His arguments were refuted by the Genevan ministers, including detailed refutations of objectionable passages from Servetus's earlier works which Servetus defended vehemently if less adequately. It was upon Servetus's interpretation of the Trinity that the case of blasphemy rested and blasphemy was punishable by death. But blasphemy was difficult to demonstrate to everyone's satisfaction and there were difficulties with proceedings against an alien visitor to the city who was not a Genevan inhabitant. However, as the trial proceeded Calvin became more convinced that it was vital to secure a conviction. After a widespread consultation of the ministers of the other Swiss Churches, they eventually passed a sentence of guilt upon Servetus on 27 October 1553. Calvin made no attempt to prevent the condemnation although he claimed that he did try to alter the method of death without success. Servetus was burnt by order of the government, suffering agonies and dying with the words; 'Jesus, Son of the Eternal God, have mercy upon me' on his lips. The trial and death haunted Calvin for the rest of his life. He took every opportunity after 1553 to refute Servetus' views. There was, in fact, little support for them amongst mainstream reformed opinion, although they did continue to have a certain currency amongst exiled refugees from Spain and Italy. One of these refugees, Matteo Gribaldi, was banished from Geneva four years later for the same heresy (but not the blasphemy) that Servetus had espoused. Another of them, Lelius Socinus (Lelio Socino), took refuge in Geneva in the same year that Servetus was burned, and professed the same anti-Trinitarian views. Later, his nephew, Faustus Socinus, was to study his uncle's manuscripts in Basel and spread anti-Trinitarian notions ('socinianism') amongst the Anabaptist brethren in Poland.

115   The *Restoration of Christianity*

Calvin's efforts to have the book destroyed at Lyons and in Frankfurt (*see below* no. 119) ensured that almost none of the original copies survived. One printed copy – that, ironically, of Calvin's colleague as a pastor in Geneva, Nicolas Colladan – did escape destruction and, after two centuries, was eventually reprinted at Nuremberg in 1790. The book is long and diffuse in character, not readily susceptible of quotation. The following passage, taken from Book IV, gives a brief glimpse of Servetus's pattern of thought.

'The divine has descended to the human so that the human might ascend to the divine'. Our inward man is nothing other than Christ himself, which is not to say that we are equal to Christ: in fact we are not equal one to another. For, as stars differ in brightness now, so shall it be at the resurrection from the dead. But Christ communicates his glory to us and we should acknowledge it as his. . . . 'The glory that you have given me I have given to them so that I may be in them as you, Father, are in me' (John 17, 6–8). Christ is called our inward man, not for simplicity's sake, but because he communicates to us his spirit by which we are renewed from day to day (2 Cor. 4; Eph. 4). . . . The more Christ renews our spirit by the fire of his spirit the more he enters into our body and the more our inward man may be said to grow in him. Our inward man consists of a divine element from Christ and a human element from our own nature so that it can truly be said that we are participants of the divine nature and that our life is hidden in that of Christ. Oh, glory incomparable! Incomparable celestial gift! Will not God's kingdom be in us if Christ who is in heaven is in us, changing us into that which he is? Our inward man is truly heavenly, having come down from heaven, of the substance of God, of the divine substance of Christ, not of blood, or of the will of the flesh but of God. . . . This truth was set out when it was said 'I tell you, you are Gods'. This is what Zachariah also predicted (Zach. 11). For just as the presence of the one God in many persons makes them divine, so the one Christ in many of us makes us both Christlike and divine.

Servetus, *Restitutio Christianismi*
(Nuremberg, 1790), pp. 558–9

116 Calvin's initial reactions

Calvin to Jean Frellon, 13 February 1547
I had great hopes of late that I could be of some use to a certain person, judging from the state of mind that I find him in; but in order to try once more to see if I can win him back to the right path, he must become another man entirely through changes that God alone can work in him. He has written to me in such a proud tone that I have tried to beat down his pride a little, speaking to him more sharply than I generally do, but I had little other choice. For I do assure you that there is no lesson more necessary for this man to learn than that of humility.

CR XL, col. 281

Calvin to Guillaume Farel, 13 February 1547
Servetus has recently written to me and has included with his letter a large volume of his wild imaginings, adding with a boastful gesture that I should find some of the contents amazing [*stupenda*] and never heard of before. If it is agreeable to me, he takes it upon himself to come here. But I am unwilling to guarantee his safety, for if he does come and my authority counts for anything, I will never let him get away alive.

CR XL, col. 283

117 Alerting the Inquisition

Guillaume Trie to Antoine Arneys, 26 February 1553
A certain heretic is countenanced among you, who ought to be burned alive, wherever he is to be found. And when I say heretic, I mean a man who will be condemned by papists as readily as he is (or should be) by ourselves. For, although we differ over many things, we agree in our belief that in the one essence of God there are three persons, and that his Son who is Eternal Wisdom was begotten by the Father before all time, and has had imparted to him his eternal virtue, which is the Holy Spirit. But when a man appears who calls the Trinity we all believe in a Cerberus and monster of hell who disgorges all the villainies it is possible to conceive of, against everything scripture teaches of the eternal generation of the Son of God, and mocks as well open-mouthed all that the ancient doctors of the Church have said – I ask you what would you do with such a man? . . . All the same there is now one living among

you who calls Jesus Christ an idol; who gathers together all the vain imaginings of the heretics of the past; who would destroy the fundamentals of the faith; who would condemn the baptism of little children and call the service a diabolical invention. . . . He is a Spanish Portuguese whose real name is Michael Servetus but who now calls himself Villeneuve and practises as a doctor. He lived for some time in Lyons and is now in Vienne, where his book has been printed by one who calls himself Balthasar Arnoullet. To prove my words I am sending the first page as evidence. You make out that books that contain nothing else but pure scripture are poison to the world. . . . Yet you tolerate poison that would obliterate Holy Writ and everything you hold dear as Christians.

CR XXXVI, cols. 837–8

118   Servetus recognized in Geneva

Theodore Beza to Heinrich Bullinger, 27 August 1553
You have doubtless heard of that impious blasphemer Servetus. He caused a book, or rather a compendium, of blasphemies to be printed secretly in Lyons. Certain good brethren at Lyons informed the magistrate of this deceitful action. Persons were despatched to Vienne, where he was practising as a physician, to bring him bound to Lyons. He was seized, but soon afterwards escaped by trickery. At length he came to Geneva, where he went prowling about. He was immediately recognized, however, by somebody and cast into prison. Calvin also, whom he treated very unhandsomely in 30 printed letters, pleaded the cause of the Church against him in the council in the presence of a great assembly of the pious, but he continued in his impiety. What will come of it I know not. Let us pray that the Lord will purge his Church of these monsters.

CR XLII, cols. 601–2

119   Attempts to prevent his book being sold

Calvin to the pastors in Frankfurt, 27 August 1553
To His dearly beloved, the pastors of the Church at Frankfurt
    You have doubtless heard of the name of Servetus, a Spaniard who 20 years ago corrupted your Germany with a virulent publication,

filled with many pernicious errors. This worthless fellow, after being driven out of Germany, and having concealed himself in France under a fictitious name, lately cobbled together a larger volume, partly from his former work and partly from new bits which he had invented. This book he secretly printed at Vienne, a town in the neighbourhood of Lyons. Many copies of it have been conveyed to Frankfurt for the Easter fair; the printer's agent, however, a pious and worthy man, on being informed that it contained nothing but a farrago of errors, suppressed whatever he had of it. It would take too long to tell you the many mistakes – and prodigious blasphemies against God – with which the book is filled. Imagine a compendium of the impious ravings of all ages. There is no sort of impiety which this monster has not raked up, as if from the infernal regions. I had rather you should pass sentence upon the book for yourselves. You will certainly find on almost every single page, what will inspire you with horror. The author himself is held in prison by our magistrates, and he will be punished before long, I trust. But it is your duty to see to it that this pestilential poison does not spread any further. The messenger will inform you of the number and location of the books.

CR XLII, cols. 599–600

120 Servetus condemned to death

Calvin to Farel, 26 October 1553
There was unanimous agreement that the wicked errors of Servetus, with which Satan formerly disturbed the Church, repeated and monstrous, were not now to be tolerated. Those of Basel agreed; those from Zurich were most emphatic of all in their approval. The serious nature of this attack on religion was accepted by them and they urged severity on our government. Those of Schaffhausen agreed. The stage Caesar, who for three days had pretended to be ill, finally faced the court to receive the penalty for his crimes. He had the nerve to ask that the matter should come before the council of 200. He was however unanimously condemned. Tomorrow he is to be brought to execution. We have tried in vain to alter the manner of his death. Why we were unsuccessful I may be able to tell you later.

CR XLII, col. 657

Calvin had a last, painful interview with Servetus two hours before he died and later recounted it in his justification for his conduct in the Servetus affair

When he [Servetus] was asked what he had to say to me, he replied that he desired to beg my pardon. Then I protested simply, and it is the truth, that I had never entertained any personal rancour against him. I reminded him gently how I had risked my life more than 16 years ago to gain him for our Saviour [see above p. 9]. If he would return to reason I would faithfully do my best to reconcile him to all good servants of God. And although he had avoided the contest I had never ceased to remonstrate with him kindly in letters. In a word, I had used all humanity to the very end, until he, being embittered by my good advice, hurled all manner of rage and anger against me. Furthermore I told him that I would pass over everything which concerned me personally. He should rather ask pardon of God whom he had so basely blasphemed in his attempt to efface the three persons in the one essence, saying that those who recognize a real distinction in one God, the Father, Son and Holy Spirit, create a three-headed hound of hell. I told him to beg the pardon of the Son of God, whom he had disfigured with his dreams, denying that he came in our flesh and was like us in his human nature, and so denying that he was our Saviour. But when I saw that all this did no good I did not wish to be wiser than my master allows. So, following the rule of St Paul, I withdrew from the heretic who was self-condemned.

CR XXXVI, col. 826

From the registers of the company of pastors, 27 October 1553
Their Lordships, having received the opinions of the Churches of Berne, Basel, Zurich and Schaffhausen upon the Servetus affair, condemned the said Servetus to be led to Champey and there to be burned alive. This was done without the said Servetus having displayed at his death any sign of repentance of his errors.

CR XXXVI, col. 830

121   Calvin's justification

A year later Calvin produced a book defending himself, the conduct of the trial and the duty of magistrates to employ their authority to maintain the faith (*The Defence of the Faith and Refutation of the Errors of Michael Servetus*, 1554). He gained some notable adverse comments from it but also much support from other reformers in Europe.

Calvin to Bullinger, 29 April 1554
In my little treatise . . . my principal and only aim was to make manifest the detestable impiety of Servetus. . . . You yourself, from your affection towards me, and the natural candour and equity of your temper, judge with indulgence. Others speak with greater harshness, saying that I am, in fact, a master of cruelty and atrocity – that I now mangle with my pen the dead man who perished at my hands. There are others who, not ill-disposed towards me, wish I had never touched on the question of the punishment of heretics. They say that others, in order to avoid public odium, have expressly held their tongues.

CR XLIII, cols. 123–4

Melanchthon to Calvin, 14 October 1554
I have read the writing in which you have refuted the detestable blasphemies of Servetus, and I give thanks to the Son of God who was the arbiter of your combat. To you, also, the Church owes, and will owe in the future, gratitude. I entirely agree with your judgement. I accept also that your magistrates have acted justly in putting this blasphemer to death after a properly conducted trial.

CR XLIII, col. 268

VI Spreading the Word

A Pamphlets

The small treatise, or pamphlet, remained one of Calvin's most effective means of conveying his message to a wider audience. Many of these tracts were composed in French; others were later translated into French from Latin. They established a new standard for vernacular literature in that genre and language. They were generally printed at Geneva, initially on the presses of Jean Girard, practically the only printer at work in the city for the first two decades of the city's reformation. Then, around 1550, many printers arrived in Geneva among the religious refugees, especially Conrad Badius, Robert Estienne (the famous royal printer from Paris), Thomas Courteau and Philibert Hamelin. By the eve of the French civil wars, Genevan printers were numerous and very busy (there are over 40 extant titles for 1561 alone). Calvin resented the time that his pamphlets took to compose, and they were never as popular in the market-place as the published sermons, but they were invariably written with great care. He lined up his targets for destructive criticism with infallible accuracy and subjected them to a merciless logic, while generally preserving an icily moderate tone. He never talked down to his audience and preferred irony to personal abuse.

Amongst the earliest was the *Treatise on Relics*, first published in 1543 and then re-issued five times in French before the end of the century. Calvin's target was the mania for collecting relics in the late-medieval Church. Relics had become ritual objects which were supposed to play a part in interceding on people's behalf before God and providing a channel for his mercy and forgiveness. Calvin had already presented his theological objections to this custom, namely, that it lacked biblical authority and led to idolatry. These views were crisply summarized before the main part of the treatise which was a catalogue of relics to be found in more than one place. The list spoke for itself. If two (or more) places claimed to have the same relic, then at least one must be a forgery. If there were so many forgeries, should any of them be trusted?

His pamphlet *Against the Anabaptists* of 1544 was a response to an invitation issued to him by the town of Neuchâtel after a public disputation which had been held in their city involving an Anabaptist. Calvin had realized the extent of Anabaptist beliefs whilst he had been resident in Strasbourg and he took the opportunity presented to him to range widely against all spiritual Anabaptists or libertine free-thinkers of various sorts. Calvin stressed that Anabaptism was contrary to all properly constituted authority. He rejected allegorical interpretations of scripture when they interpreted them less modestly than he did. He reassessed the proper use of excommunication, the civil authority of the magistrate and the use of the Christian oath.

In the same year, Calvin also launched another polemic against 'fellow-travellers' in the Reformation. His criticism of the hypocrites who made a virtue of their refusal to support the cause openly made Calvin appear (especially in France, where persecution had become more rigorous) the champion of a demanding and uncompromising faith. He especially aimed his remarks at courtiers, intellectuals and businessmen – those who could afford to stand up in public for the faith which they toyed with in private. The pamphlet ensured that the term 'nicodemite' became a term of abuse in frequent use during the French civil wars.

Calvin's most sustained invective was directed towards the Roman Catholic Church's own efforts at reform. His long pamphlet *On the Necessity of Reforming the Church* (1544) was a critique of its early attempts to re-unite Christendom which led, eventually, to the calling of the council of Trent in 1545. After the first seven sessions there, it transferred to Bologna, and this gave Calvin (whose views had never been referred to during its debates) an opportunity to write the first Protestant commentary on it. In a long tract, completed in November 1547 (*The Acts of the Council of Trent with the Antidote*), Calvin commented on every important published account of the speeches and conclusions they had reached. He ridiculed the qualifications of those who had attended it, their procedures, and he ended with a re-statement of what reformation was really about.

122   *On Relics* (1543)

Let us begin then with Christ. As his natural body could not be possessed (though some people have found it easy to fabricate numerous
miraculous bodies for him to please themselves) they have collected
instead 600 frivolous items to compensate for its absence. The body of
Christ has not been allowed to escape entirely. For, besides some teeth
and hair, the monks of Charroux claim to have his prepuce, that is, his
foreskin cut off during his circumcision. How, one may ask, did this
foreskin get there? The Evangelist Luke states that the Lord was
circumcized but nowhere says that the skin was preserved as a relic. All
the ancient histories are silent about it and for 500 years this subject
was not once mentioned in the Christian Church. Why was it hidden
for all that time and how did it come to travel as far as Charroux? As a
proof of its authenticity, they say that some drops of blood have been
seen to fall from it. They indeed say that, but they should prove it. It is
plainly an absurdity. Even if we were to accept that this foreskin had
been preserved and so might be there or elsewhere, what shall we say
about the foreskin shown in Rome at the church of John Lateran? As it
is certain that there was only one of them, it cannot possibly be both in
Rome and in Charroux. Thus the falsehood becomes manifest.

At the end of the treatise, Calvin recalls an incident from his childhood at
Noyon.

When this little book was passing through the press, I was informed of a
third foreskin, which I had not mentioned, and which is displayed at
Hildesheim. The number of similar follies is indeed infinite and a careful inspection would discover more than it is possible to enumerate. Let
every one, then, be on guard, not allowing themselves to be led like
mindless animals as if they could not make out the way or path that
might be the right one. I recollect when I was a boy how they were
accustomed to treat images in our parish. When the feast of Stephen
drew near, they adorned the statues all alike with garlands and
necklaces, decorating the murderers who stoned Stephen in the same
way as they decorated Stephen himself. When the old women saw the
murderers thus adorned they imagined that these statues were the
companions of Stephen. Accordingly every one of them was presented
with a candle. The same honour was even conferred on the devil who
contended with Michael, and so on with the rest of them. So completely
are they all mixed up together that it is impossible to have the bones of a
martyr without running the risk of having the bones of a thief or

robber, or even those of a dog, horse or donkey. The Virgin Mary's comb, ring or girdle cannot be venerated without the risk of paying homage to some prostitute's clothing. Let those who are inclined in this direction be warned. Henceforth no one will be able to excuse himself on the grounds of ignorance.

CR XXXIV, cols. 415, 452

123   *Against the Anabaptists* (1544)

The Anabaptists can be divided into two principal sects of which the first, whilst full of errors, malice and wickedness, is none the less the more straightforward. Its adherents at least accept holy scripture; if you argue with them you know where your differences lie, for they make themselves understood and you know where you can agree with them and where you disagree. The second group exists in a labyrinth of incredible dreams so that it is astonishing that any creature resembling a human being can be so devoid of human reasoning as to allow itself to be deceived into believing these monstrous fantasies. Members of this sect are called the libertines. They counterfeit the spiritual world and take no account of the holy Word of God (registering it as a fairy tale) unless it happens (or can be twisted) to fit their own diabolical opinions. They have another characteristic, which they share with wayside tramps, namely that you cannot make out what they are trying to say or what they mean – that is unless by this device they are shrewdly trying to cover up the grossness of their beliefs. For their intention is chiefly to remove the difference between good and evil, to mix up God and the Devil so that you cannot recognize one from the other, thus making men confused before God and their own consciences as well as impudent before the world. . . .

They [Anabaptists] conclude that all use of weapons is diabolical. Now it is true that the individual's use of force to resist evil is not permissible, for the Christian's weapons are prayer and suffering, and his life is one of patient conquest of evil by good as the Evangelist has commanded (Luke 21, 19; Romans 12, 21). . . . But to condemn the use of public force of arms which God has instructed us to use for our protection is a blasphemy against God himself. The spirit of God was pronounced through St Paul when he said that the magistrate was a minister of God to prevent violence and repress wickedness amongst us to our benefit and advantage (Romans 13, 4). For this reason he has been endowed with a sword to punish wrongdoing. What God has ordained we should not prohibit. . . .

Besides, it is certain that these poor deluded folk intend to condemn all fortifications, armaments, armour and such things for the defence of a country, and to persuade subjects to disobey their princes and superiors when they ask for assistance in an emergency. But to disapprove of something that our Lord never disapproved of is to go beyond our authority as mortal men. To hold to such opinions is to usurp God's authority by condemning that which he has permitted. . . .

[The Anabaptists] have honoured principalities and lordships with the name of brigandage. But seeing that they could not defend this position they have quietly retreated, using as a screen the argument that, according to God's ordinances, earthly dominion is incompatible with Christ's perfection. But by this they imply that it is a forbidden estate and closed to all Christians. . . . We have thus to investigate whether Christianity is compatible with the exercise of justice or earthly dominion. . . . How is it that the judges in the Old Testament, the good kings such as David, Hezekiah, Josiah and even some of the prophets exercised their authority? . . . David's rule earned not just God's approval but also his praise and the bestowal of many noble titles. . . . There is no other refuge for these enemies of all good order than to argue that Our Lord required a greater perfection of the Christian Church than he did of the Jewish people. This might be true in the matter of rituals. But it is a false opinion that we should have to abide by a different moral order. . . . In fact it would be absurd for the magnificent and exalted vocation of ruler to be denied to some one who was a Christian. St Paul calls upon every Christian to stick to his calling (1 Corinthians 7, 20). Shepherds, labourers in the fields, artisans and others are called holy and not prohibited on the grounds of Christian perfection. We should now ask which calling is most approved of by God, the leader of sheep or of men. . . . Could you ask for greater praise for a vocation than that the Lord should call it divine (Psalms 82, 6)? If this title is given to a prince, who would dare to say that it is not worthy of a faithful Christian? . . .

Jesus Christ, they [the Anabaptists] say, declined to undertake the division of the possessions between the two brothers in Luke 12, 4. [To them] it follows that a Christian should not become involved in civil law suits as a judge. But, firstly, St Paul lets Christians do what Jesus Christ refused to do in this passage (1 Corinthians 6, 1). . . . And further, if a Christian is not permitted to take part in the settling of law suits concerning possessions, inheritance and other wealth, what, I ask these good doctors, will become of the world? . . . It is easy to see that these wretched feather-brained individuals tend only in one direction, which is to put all to disorder and have all goods in common such that whoever can grab the most will be praised. They may deny any such intention now. But if one removes all the laws and arbitrators from the world, as they intend and strictly demand, what will result except an unrestrained brigandage?

CR XXXV, cols. 53–4, 77–8, 80–7

124   *Apology to the Nicodemites* (1544)

There are some people who reckon that I am too harsh, and complain because I treat them too brutally. If you ask them the reason for their dissatisfaction it is that they cannot bear to be hurt. This is what they complain about, not that I condemn them for being wrong. Their sole comfort is this miserable deceit: that their inward heart believes in the Lord whatever outwardly appears to be the case. What is there to be said? They are split between God and the Devil, giving their souls to the one and their bodies to the other. Their hearts, at least (as they say), are the Lord's, but they rest content that they dabble in profane and wicked things. Will God, I ask you, be satisfied with such a position? Will he who said that every knee should bow, and every tongue should confess his name, now let you kneel before false gods? Our doctrine, as I have said, is clear and easy to accept or reject if it is the truth that you are after. . . .

I am not speaking generally about all those whose infirmities keep them chained to this Babylonian captivity in which they are polluted with idolatrous superstition. Many know it in their hearts, confess their lack of courage, are saddened by it, and pray incessantly to God for strength and for mercy. I am talking about those who look out for every possible subterfuge to hide behind, who laugh when they are told about it, or become bitter, even taking the Lord's name in vain. This is why they have taken the name of Nicodemus as their defence, as though they were his disciples. I will call them Nicodemites for the moment, until I have shown how greatly they slander this holy person by putting him amongst their number. . . .

Nicodemites are not all of one kind. . . . The first are those who, to gain some credit, profess to preach the Word and give a few tastes of it to attract people. They know that a large number of people are now bored by the old-fashioned, panting efforts of preachers, and make fun of this way of sermonizing. They see no better way of gaining a reputation and fame than by using the reform as a bait to draw the crowd to them. Their intention is, however, to abuse God's Word and to utilize it merely to gain a benefice or otherwise enrich themselves. . . . There is a second sort. These are refined diplomats. They are quite enchanted with the Word, will discuss it endlessly with the ladies, providing that it does not ask them to change their lives. The courtiers and courtesans I put in the same bracket for they are more concerned that no one should offend their exquisite good taste. I am not surprised that they should plot against me as though I had planned to attack them, since they are offended by my austerity. . . . The third sort are those who have half turned Christianity into a philosophy. At any rate they do not take much to heart but wait and see if there is to be (without contributing much to it themselves) a solid reformation. They have no stomach for it themselves, for they can see that it is something rather dangerous. More especially, some among them are Platonists, with their heads so full of his ideas of the way to serve God that, as a result, they ignore most of the foolish superstitions of the papacy as things beyond their concern. These are nearly all men of letters, although not all writers are like this. I would prefer all human knowledge to be wiped off the face of the earth than that it should become the cause for the loss of faith amongst Christians or a cause for their turning against God. . . . In the fourth category fall the merchants and common people who are ensconced in their family lives and do not thank you for disturbing their routines. Thus, since it seems to them that I do not have sufficient regard for their creature comforts, they also refuse to have me for their teacher. They prudently imagine that they will be acquitted before God if they deny what I preach. . . .

I ask all these people how they can say (whatever their motives) that I am too extreme. For I merely tell them the things that their own consciences tell them are wicked and damnable and manifest idolatry. I speak what scripture says. I do not decide things in a hurry and always reflect at least three times upon them. And finally, what I say is so manifestly true that no one can deny it without denying the Word of God.

CR XXXIV, cols. 594–602

125 *Against the Council of Trent* (1547)

Perhaps 40 bishops or so are present. I do not know the exact number or care very much about it, for it is of little consequence. . . . Were one to conduct a review of them, how many of them would pass muster? For, when the venerable fathers look at each other, it must be impossible for them not to feel ashamed; for they know and cannot be ignorant of the opinion which they have of each other. Hence, if you took away the name of council, the whole papacy would have to confess that all the bishops who attended were nothing but the dregs. . . .

Even if their regulations had been perfect in every way, good men could not congratulate themselves on the prospect of better things to come. For, before deciding anything else, the members of the council shattered the possibility of progress being made, or at least showed a way by which it could be effectively impeded. For they promised that none of their ensuing decisions should hinder the Apostolic See from maintaining its authority unimpaired. Consider, now, how extensive this authority is and how little it is limited. Does not a preliminary decision of this kind mean, in effect, that popes may order anything to be lawful as they please? None of these things which they undertake to correct has hitherto been practised as if permitted by common laws, but what the laws prohibited has been permitted without redress by means of papal dispensations. . . .

I will waste no further time exposing their impudence. But, as all can see, they are worse than useless; any one who is wise will, in future, take no notice of their decrees and be in no doubt about it. It would be most desirable, indeed, if the dissensions currently disturbing the Church could be settled by the authority of a pious council, but, as matters stand, this cannot be hoped for. Therefore, since Churches are scattered in a dreadful way, and no hope of gathering them together appears from mankind, we cannot do better than hasten to rally round the banner which the Son of God holds out for us. This is not the time to keep waiting for each other. As each person sees the light of scripture beaming forth, let him follow it immediately. As for the whole body of the Church, we commend it to the care of the Lord.

CR XXXV, cols. 382, 504–6

B Preaching and Teaching

Much of Calvin's time in Geneva was spent in preaching sermons and giving lectures. Prior to 1549 he gave three sermons during the week at five o'clock in the evenings and also preached three times on Sundays. After 1549 he preached every weekday in each alternate week and then twice on Sundays. His lectures were delivered to the Friday congregation, or company, of pastors and, later, before the Academy of Geneva (*See below* pp. 124–7). In his lecturing and preaching Calvin based himself on the original biblical texts (in Hebrew for the Old Testament and Greek for the New) and took it as his task to expound the text clearly and concisely without overburdening it with references or fitting it into a predetermined methodology. His style was perfected while he was at Strasbourg. The preface to his first published commentary in 1540 – that on St Paul's letters to the Romans – reveals that he had carefully considered his styles of commentary.

The process of producing printed commentaries was much assisted when, perhaps in 1552, an elaborate system of stenography was devised by the pastors of the congregation so that Calvin could deliver his lectures and then have a draft of what he had said to revise for publication. For his sermons, the company of exiles [*compagnie des estrangers*] provided a stenographer in 1549, Denis Raguenier, who devised a shorthand which enabled him to take down single-handed Calvin's sermons. Initially these were copied into folio volumes and entrusted to the care of the deacons for anyone who wanted to read them. Later some of them were published and many were translated, especially into English. A copy of Calvin's sermons on Ephesians was later found at the bedside of John Knox after his death in 1572. As a result of Raguenier's labours, there are now, in manuscript or in print, over 2,000 of Calvin's sermons. They are the authentic tone of the reformer, speaking a plain, colloquial but metropolitan French, and ranging over, as he spoke, all the issues of his day.

126 Scriptural interpretation

The scriptures obtain full authority among believers only when men regard them as having sprung from heaven, as if the living voices of God were heard there.

Institutes I, vii, 1

Man is united to Christ through the Holy Spirit, who is co-eternal, revealed to man by faith, through whom Christ's bodily presence may be partaken. It was through the Holy Spirit, inspiring the prophets and evangelists, that God spoke to man through the scriptures of which he is the author. The children of God 'know no other Spirit than him who dwelt and spoke in the apostles, and by whose oracles they are continually recalled to the hearing of the Word'.

Institutes I, ix, 3

Let the reader remember to read the whole narrative together and to draw the inference, not from single parts, but from the whole.

Galatians, p. 40

Calvin to Viret, 19 May 1540
Capito has some things in his lectures which may be useful to you in illustrating Isaiah.[1] But he does not read it [from a text] to his audience and has, moreover, not yet reached chapter 14, so he will not help you much at present. Zwingli does not lack an apt and ready exposition, but he takes too many liberties and therefore often strays far from the prophet's meaning. Luther does not worry much about how he expresses things or about historical accuracy either. He is content to elicit a fruitful meaning. I think no one has applied himself more diligently to this task than Oecolampadius, though he has not always arrived at the full scope of meaning.

CR XXXIX, col. 36

127 Times for preaching in Geneva

24 October 1549, council of 24
The honoured minister Calvin. He was asked to advise concerning a proposal to preach each morning and whether he would feel overburdened. He gave his opinion. It was decided that the preachers should preach each morning. . . .

CR XLIX, col. 457

---

[1] Viret was in process of preparing a commentary on Isaiah. Capito, principal minister in Strasbourg, was lecturing on it.

128   Copying of lectures and sermons

About this same time the task of taking down his lectures and writing
them out word for word was begun. It is true that several people had
tried to do this already, both with his lectures and his sermons; but they
had not reached the point of being able to take it all down accurately,
but had only extracted the principal points and not followed the matter
through completely and in order. Nevertheless, what these pioneers
did certainly deserved praise . . . for they gave the others the
opportunity for going further and, so to speak, perfecting the business.
It was a great gift from God in M. Jean Budé, Charles de Jonvillier and
Denis Raguenier, for by means of the freely-given labours of the first
two we have the lectures of this good servant of God, and by means of
the third, paid for by the company of exiles, his sermons. . . .

> *CR* XLIX, cols. 70–1 (Colladon, *Life of Calvin*, 1565)

129   Social Comment

Few subjects of contemporary interest escape Calvin's attention during his
sermons and lectures. The following is a short, random selection:

Women have been allowed for a long time to become increasingly
audacious. And besides, speech apart, they wear such provocative
clothes that it is hard to discern whether they are women or men. They
appear in new dresses and trinkets, so that some new disguise is daily to
be seen. They come decked out in peacock-tail fashion, so that a man
cannot pass within three feet of them without feeling, as it were, a
windmill sail swirling past him. Ribald songs, too, are part of their
behaviour. . . .

> *Ephesians*, p. 497

When the Lord afflicts a country with war or famine, the rich make
great gain by such evils. They abuse the scourge of God; for we see
merchants getting rich in the midst of wars, inasmuch as they scrape
together a booty from every quarter. For those who wage war are
forced to borrow cash, as also the peasants and mechanics, so that they
can pay their taxes; and then, so that they can live, they are obliged to
make unjust agreements; thus the increase in wealth. Those in

authority also, and in favour at the court of princes, gain more from wars, famine and other calamities than during times of peace and prosperity; for when peace flourishes, the state of things is then more equable; but when the poor are burdened the rest grow fat.

Minor Prophets (Joel) I, pp. 300–1

Learning and the liberal arts were not, then, so despised as they are in this age, and in those immediately preceding it. So strongly has barbarism prevailed in the world that it is almost a disgrace for nobles to be reckoned among the men of education and of letters! The chief boast of the nobility was to be destitute of scholarship – nay, they gloried in the assertion that they were 'no scholars' as they put it; and if any of their rank were versed in literature, they acquired their attainments for no other purpose than to be made bishops and abbots.

Daniel, pp. 90–1

This is similar to that of the Turks today, were they to invade these parts and exercise their authority. For, you might ask the French kings and their counsellors, 'Whose fault is it that the Turks come to us so easily? It is because you have prepared the way for them by sea, because you have bribed them, and because your ports have been open to them; and yet they have wilfully exercised the greatest cruelty towards your subjects'.

Jeremiah II, pp. 187–8

We see how great is the folly of those who are desirous to have a powerful and wealthy king reigning over them, and how justly they are punished for their ambition, though it cannot be corrected by the experience of every day, which is everywhere seen in the world. France and Spain, at the present, boast that they are governed by mighty princes, but feel to their cost how little advantage they derive from that which dazzles them by a false pretence of honour.

Isaiah II, p. 54

C Exiles and Refugees

In 1557 the council of the city ordered all the city's inhabitants to
assemble for a full-dress military parade. But the order was subsequently rescinded when it was objected that there would be more
foreigners than native Genevans participating in the review. The wave
of exiles and refugees to Geneva began about 1542 and increased with
the gathering persecution in Italy and parts of France. In 1549 the city
council began keeping a register of all refugees arriving newly to the
city along the routes from Lyons, Burgundy and Turin, and recording
their place of origin.[2] From 1549 to January 1560 this *Livre des Habitants*
enables historians to measure the number of new arrivals year by year.
Allowing for those who left Geneva for other destinations of exile, it
has been estimated that Geneva probably received about 7,000
immigrants between 1550 and 1562. They came mainly from French-
speaking parts of Europe, but there were also separate Italian and
English minorities. They organized their own meetings and welfare,
and Calvin became worried in the early 1550s at the difficulties of
absorbing the numbers of refugees. In fact they were small then in
comparison with those arriving after 1557, when, as a result of the
persecution in France and the Low Countries, they reached their peak.
It was, perhaps, inevitable that there would develop an exaggerated
respect amongst the refugees for the Genevan Church. Calvin had
even to urge Calvinists abroad not to regard Geneva as a kind of second
Rome.

130 Exiles from Provence (1545)

This year [1545] was also infamous for the savage butchery that the
judges at Aix perpetrated upon the Waldensian brethren of Mérindol
and Cabrier and the whole of that district – not upon one or two individuals, but upon the whole population, without distinction of age or
sex, burning down their villages as well. These calamities affected
Calvin the more deeply, when consoling and refreshing those who took
refuge in Geneva, because he had formerly taken care by letters and by
supplying them with pastors to have them purely instructed in the

---

[2] A map, based on the information in this register for France, showing the geograph-
ical location of the origins of refugees in Geneva at this period, can be found *inter alia* in
W. Monter, *Calvin's Geneva* (New York, 1967) p. 168.

gospel; and when they had formerly been threatened he had saved
them by interceding for them with the princes of Germany and the
cantons.

CR XLIX, col. 136

131   Exiles arriving in large numbers (1551)

Calvin to Guillaume Farel, 15 June 1551
I am, meanwhile, much preoccupied with the foreigners who daily pass
through this place in great numbers, or who have come here to live.
Among others, the marquis de Vico, a Neapolitan, arrived recently.[3]
Another will follow shortly. Should you pay us a visit next autumn, you
will find our city considerably increased – a pleasing spectacle to me, if
they do not overwhelm me with their visits.

CR XLII, col. 134

132   Foreigners' bursary

Calvin to Guillaume Farel, 30 December 1553
Good men have sent money to be spent upon the banished brethren
and exiles. They have ordered one part of it to be distributed amongst
those here, and have designated the other two parts for the poor at
Lausanne and your own city [Neuchâtel]. Our friend Beza has
arranged for 25 gold pieces to be handed over to them. However, since
very few exiles have so far gone to stay with you, so far as I know,
especially of that sort which is so numerous here, would you not, if you
are not in immediate need, put yours towards the relief of others in
need?

CR XLII, cols. 723-4

133   Easter refugees (1554)

Calvin to Heinrich Bullinger, 28 March 1554
An immense number of men, disregarding the rumours in France
about our disturbances[4], have flocked here from all quarters to

---

[3] Galeas Caraccioli, marquis of Vico, a Neapolitan noble converted to the reformed
faith by Peter Martyr and registered as an inhabitant on 15 June 1551.
[4] *See above,* p. 90.

celebrate Easter. Though the king [of France] stationed guards to watch all the passes, and his lieutenants execute most punctually all his orders . . . nevertheless, the ardour of their piety has triumphed over all fears to such a degree that good men break through every obstacle.

CR XLIII, col. 94

134   John Knox's admiration for Geneva

John Knox to Mrs Anne Locke, Geneva, 9 December 1556
This place . . . is the maist perfyt schoole of Chryst that ever was in the erth since the dayis of the Apostillis. In other places, I confess Chryst to be trewlie preachit; but maneris and religioun so sinceirlie reformat, I have not yit sene in any other place; besydes, Sathan, I confess, rageth aganis the ane and the other, but potent is He that hath promissit to be with us in all suche interprises as we tak in hand at his commandement, for the glorie of his name and for mantenance of his trew religioun; and thairfoir the less we feir any contrare power, yea, in the boldness of our God we altogither contempn thame, be thai kingis, emperours, men, angellis, or devillis, for thai salbe never abill to prevale against the simpill treuth of God whilk we oppinlie profess. Be the permissioun of God, thai may appeir to prevale aganis our bodies, but our cause sall triumphe in dispyt of Sathan.

The Works of John Knox, ed. D. Laing (4 vols., Edinburgh, 1855) IV, pp. 240–1

D Geneva's Academy

Calvin's ordinances for Geneva had already envisaged the importance of the Genevan academy for training scholars in the Reformation and producing Calvinist preachers (*see above* p. 73). It was only in 1558 that Calvin's intentions were fully realized. Secondary education had indeed been maintained throughout the Reformation at the small *collège* de Rive with a frequently absentee headmaster and some assistant masters who taught the elements of Latin to undisciplined pupils in decaying buildings. After a careful inspection in 1555, it was apparent that new buildings, new teachers and a fresh curriculum were urgently needed. By 1558 all these had been provided. The college

(*schola privata*), the equivalent of a secondary school, now had a
headmaster (*ludi magister*) who also taught the first (or senior) class in
dialectic, rhetoric and declamation from the speeches of Cicero and
Demosthenes. In addition, seven teachers taught boys to read, speak
and write good Latin and Greek. School began at 6 a.m. in the summer
and 7 a.m. in the winter. Wednesdays were entirely devoted to
religious instruction, attendance at a sermon, tutorials and
preparation. Punctuality, order, industry, were the qualities most
needed in the pupils. Inevitably a great deal of their attention was
directed to the Bible and Christian doctrine. There were no games or
times for recreation, and the only holidays were the three weeks of the
wine harvest. The school, frequently inspected, and staffed by teachers
acceptable to Calvin, produced a generation of pupils who were
serious, hardy, pious and thoroughly grounded in the classical
languages and the Bible. Its curriculum and organization owed much
to the example of the Strasbourg college, opened by the great
Protestant educationalist Jean Sturm.

Beyond the secondary school was the academy, which had many of
the characteristics of a university without any faculty of medicine or of
law. It was orientated to the study of theology and the training of men
for the service of the Church. The success of the new Genevan academy
was in part the result of differences between the government of Berne
and the clergy who staffed the academy at Lausanne, under Bernese
jurisdiction. There, Pierre Viret and other prominent pastors insisted
on teaching undiluted predestination, defied their government and
migrated to Geneva in 1558 just when their services were most needed.
With them came the ideal rector who provided the perfect link with the
college and who brought a profound knowledge of Greek together with
convictions which exactly harmonized with those of Calvin. A
Burgundian from Vézelay, alumnus of Paris, Bourges and Orléans
universities, Theodore Beza (1519–1605) was wealthy, learned and
completely devoted to Calvin. With his assistance the new Genevan
academy was able to recruit talented scholars of Greek, philosophy,
mathematics and Hebrew. It opened in June 1559, and from the
beginning attracted recruits from a wide European background.

135 College ordinances (June 1559)

The behaviour of teachers is to be suitably serious; they are not to make
derogatory remarks about the authors they are expounding, but

confine themselves to making their meaning clear. They should warn their pupils about matters that are either obscure or out of place or cannot be dealt with fully. Silence should be observed; and negligent, inattentive or disorderly pupils are to be punished. The chief aim of the teaching is to be love of God and hatred of evil. They must not leave the classroom before the end of the lesson: when the bell rings, they should depart in an orderly fashion.

The pupils must treat one another in a friendly and truly Christian manner, and there must be no quarrelling during lessons. If there is any argument it must be referred to the Rector and the case must be stated to him in a Christian way. If it is not settled satisfactorily, it is to be referred to the ministers of God's Word, who will give an authoritative ruling.

The headmaster who is chosen and appointed is to be a God-fearing man, reasonably well qualified, a man of friendly disposition, neither rough nor harsh, able to set a good example to the scholars and to deal patiently with difficulties as they arise. In addition to the ordinary class teaching, he is to care for the morals and the industry of the establishment, take notice of and reprimand any who are late, be responsible for the punishments in the assembly hall, make sure that the bell rings at the proper time, and that the pupils are neatly dressed. . . .

Lessons follow [morning assembly], lasting in summer time for an hour and a half; then they are allowed half an hour for breakfast, which is to be eaten quietly and with prayers. After that there is teaching until 9 o'clock. In winter lessons are from 7 to 9 without any break for breakfast, which is to be taken incidentally whilst pupils are working at their texts. When morning lessons are over, the Lord's Prayer is to be said in each classroom, together with grace. Then, reminding them of their work, two teachers accompany them to their homes, taking this duty in turn.

In both winter and summer the pupils return after dinner at 11 and practise singing the psalms until 12. Then a lesson follows until 1, followed, after prayers, by an hour's break; then two hours lessons until 4 o'clock. Then the bell rings for assembly in the hall where, in the presence of headmaster and teachers, punishments are administered with deliberate moderation, and three pupils say in French the Lord's Prayer, the Creed and the ten commandments. Dismissal follows, with the headmaster giving a blessing.

CR XXXVIII, cols. 69–74

136   Academy ordinances (June 1559)

The three lecturers, namely those in Hebrew, Greek and the arts, should be chosen and should accept the regulations in the same way as the school-teachers.

On Monday, Tuesday and Thursday of each week there should be two lectures given by each of them, one for an hour in the morning and the other for an hour in the afternoon. On Wednesday and Friday they should each lecture for an hour after dinner. On Saturday there shall be no lectures given. On Sunday they should go to hear the sermons.

. . . The Hebrew lecturer should comment upon some book from the Old Testament in the mornings. In the afternoons he should lecture on Hebrew grammar.

The Greek professor should lecture after the Hebrew class on some book of philosophy concerning morals. The book will be chosen from the works of Aristotle, Plato, Plutarch or one of the Christian philosophers. After lunch, he will deliver lectures . . . on some Greek poet, orator or historian, making a choice of the purest among them.

The lecturer in arts will follow the professor of Greek and he will lecture on a book of physics for half an hour. After lunch . . . he will expound knowledgeably the Rhetorics of Aristotle, the most famous speeches of Cicero or the books of Horace.

CR XXXVIII, cols. 75–80

VII Dogma and Diplomacy

Before his return to Geneva in 1541 Calvin had already been initiated into the tortuous and unrewarding activity of international theological politics. He attended the great colloquies with the Catholics, organized by the emperor Charles V in 1539–41 to end the schism of the Church. He was present at Frankfurt-am-Main in February 1539 as an assistant to Martin Bucer, the great Strasbourg theologian; his letters from Ratisbon in April–May 1541 are amongst the most revealing accounts of the failure of the great German diet held there. Calvin met for the first time the moderate Lutheran divine Philip Melanchthon. But he remained suspicious of Catholic intentions, and he later criticized the Lutherans for being prepared to make doctrinal concessions too readily. Thereafter, Calvin concentrated his personal efforts on attempting to reach a common confession of faith among the reformed Churches.

A The Agreement of Zurich (1549)

Almost 10 years of negotiations, exchanges, discussion and debate took place before the famous Agreement of Zurich (*Consensus Tigurinus*) was achieved between the Churches of Geneva, Zurich and Neuchâtel in 1549. Its 26 articles were a complete theological compromise. Its first clauses stressed the spiritual presence of the body and blood of Christ in the Eucharist (*see above* pp. 37–8), whereas its subsequent clauses reflected the Zwinglian notions of the sacraments as a mere sign of a living faith in Christ. It formed the basis of many confessions of faith drawn up for use in the reformed Churches of Scotland (1560), France (1559), Heidelberg (1563) and Poland (1557).

137 *Consensus Tigurinus* (1549)

3 Nature of the knowledge of Christ
We must hold therefore that Christ, being the eternal Son of God, and of the same essence and glory with the Father, assumed our flesh, to communicate to us by right of adoption that which he possessed by nature, namely, to make us sons of God. This is done when, ingrafted by faith into the body of Christ, and that by the agency of the Holy Spirit, we are first counted righteous by a free imputation of righteousness, and then regenerated to a new life; whereby being formed again in the image of our heavenly Father, we renounce the old self.

5 How Christ communicates himself to us
Moreover, that Christ may thus exhibit himself to us and produce these effects in us, he must be made one with us, and we must be ingrafted into his body. He does not infuse his life into us unless he is our head, and from him the whole body, fitly joined together, is supplied and, according to his working, increases the body in the proportion of each member.

6 Spiritual communion – institution of the sacraments
The spiritual communion which we have with the Son of God takes place when he, dwelling in us by his Spirit, makes all who believe capable of all the blessings which reside in him. In order to testify this, both the preaching of the gospel was appointed, and the use of the sacraments committed to us, namely, the sacraments of holy baptism and the Holy Supper.

7 The purposes of the sacraments
The purposes of the sacraments are to be marks and badges of Christian profession and fellowship or fraternity, to be incitements to gratitude and exercises of faith and a godly life; in short, to be contracts binding us to this. But among other ends the principal one is that God may, by means of them, testify, represent and seal his grace to us. For although they signify nothing else than is announced to us by the Word itself, yet it is a great matter, *first*, that there is submitted to our eyes a set of living images which make a deeper impression on the senses, by bringing the object in a manner directly before them, while they bring the death of Christ and all his benefits to our memory, that faith might be the better exercised; and, *secondly*, that what the mouth of God had announced is, as it were, confirmed and ratified by seals.

8 Gratitude

Now, seeing that these things which the Lord has given us as testimonies and seals of his grace are true, without doubt he really performs within by his Spirit that which the sacraments figure to our eyes and other senses; in other words, we obtain possession of Christ as the fountain of all blessings, both in order that we may be reconciled to God by means of his death, be renewed by his Spirit to holiness of life, in short, obtain righteousness and salvation; and also in order that we may give thanks for the blessings which were once exhibited on the cross, and which we daily receive by faith.

9 The signs and the things signified not disjoined but distinct

Wherefore, though we distinguish, as we ought, between the signs and the things signified, yet we do not disjoin the reality from the signs, but acknowledge that all who in faith embrace the promises there offered receive Christ spiritually, with his spiritual gifts, while those who had long been made partakers of Christ continue and renew that communion.

10 The promise principally to be looked to in the sacraments

And it is proper to look not to the bare signs, but rather to the promise thereto annexed. As far, therefore, as our faith in the promise there offered prevails, so far will that virtue and efficacy of which we speak display itself. Thus, the substance of water, bread and wine by no means offers Christ to us, nor makes us capable of his spiritual gifts. The promise rather is to be looked to whose office it is to lead us to Christ by the direct way of faith - faith which makes us partakers of Christ.

Tracts II, pp. 212–15

B Discussions with the Lutherans

In 1529 the conference at Marburg had failed to produce a common confession for all the reformed Churches.[1] Until Luther's death in 1546, Calvin hoped that his talks with other Swiss Churches might be widened to include the Lutherans and succeed where Marburg failed.

[1] Rupp and Drewery, *Martin Luther*, pp. 132–7; Potter, *Huldrych Zwingli* pp. 89–109.

He expressed his private hopes in a letter to a distinguished Lutheran theologian and friend to Luther and Melanchthon, Dietrich de Weit, preacher in Nuremberg. But after Luther's death, Lutheran church leaders rejected any reconciliation and the following decade was to see the failure in Calvin's lifetime of any attempt to arrive at a common confession. The Lutherans felt vulnerable after the civil war in Germany (1546–7) and constrained by the doctrinal settlement offered them by the Emperor in the Interim in June 1548. Some Lutheran pastors were upset at not being consulted before the Agreement of Zurich was reached in 1549. Finally, in a number of German cities, a reaction took place against the (largely foreign) Calvinist or Swiss-reformed congregations in their midst. This began in Strasbourg in 1554; in the same year, Hamburg gave a cold welcome to exiles from persecution in England and the Low Countries. The Lutheran pastor in Hamburg, a well-trained and vitriolic theologian called Joachim Westphal, produced the first Lutheran pamphlet to attack the propositions of the Agreement of Zurich (*The compilation of confused and divergent opinions concerning the Lord's Supper*, 1552). In this, Calvin became a cow (*das Kalbe*), Bullinger in Zurich a bull (*der Bulle*), and the leader of the exiles from England, the Polish John a Lasco, a Polish bear. To this, and other invective, Calvin wrote an initial reply in 1555 which, whilst not mentioning Westphal by name, dismissed him as a 'hothead' and a 'son of the devil'. In the following year, Calvin again wrote a pamphlet against him, although the preface, dedicated to the churches in Saxony and lower Germany, reveals his awareness that nothing fruitful could come of this acrimony. In fact, the differences between the two traditions had become too wide to bridge by a mere formula of confession. Lutheranism had become the 'official' reformed religion in Germany in the Peace of Augsburg in 1555, whilst Calvinism had been officially outlawed. Thereafter, Calvinism would establish a foothold only in certain localities in the Holy Roman Empire. Elsewhere, it became the religion of those in reaction to Lutheran Germanic culture in Poland, Hungary and the Low Countries.

138   To Theodorus Vitus (Dietrich de Weit) 17 March 1546

I am delighted that my pamphlet *On the Sacraments* [*Petit traicté de la saincte cene* . . ., 1541] has not displeased you. It was written in French 10 years ago. I agreed eventually to its publication (in Latin) when I learnt that it had been translated by two individuals already and I was afraid lest a poorer version of it should be printed. The simple and popular style of exposition in it – adapted for an unlearned audience – indicates what I originally had in mind. For I usually write more carefully for those with a knowledge of Latin. But I worked hard, nevertheless, to express my views accurately and briefly and reveal them with clarity but devoid of technicalities. . . . As you say, if only the people of Zurich would agree with this formula on the sacraments! I do not think that Luther will prove so stubborn that we cannot easily reach an agreement with him on this matter. At least my views have not been publicly condemned by him. The chief obstacle to agreement with the Lutherans is the powerful hold exercised by their preconceptions, accepted for so long that people are not prepared to consider anything new.

CR XL, col. 316

139   Preface to the *Second Defence of the holy and orthodox faith in the matter of the sacraments* (against Westphal) (1556)

To all honest ministers of Christ . . . in the churches of Saxony and lower Germany, John Calvin, with brotherly affection, wishes increase of grace from God the Father and our Lord Jesus Christ.

Although I am perfectly conscious that the cause which I have undertaken to defend in this book is right and just . . . I have thought it important, venerable and beloved brethren, to protest to you at the start that this book has been dragged from me. I would have kept silent, were I not, by that, to betray the truth of Christ, in the oppression of which ferocious men exceed the barbarism of the papacy. . . .

Most of you are well aware of the short description which we published five years ago under the name of the Agreement, in which, without attacking anyone, and without any bitterness of language, we not only arranged the substance of the whole controversy [over the sacraments] under distinct headings but also endeavoured, in so far as a candid confession of the truth allowed, entirely to remove all offences. . . . We also promised that we would be open to instruction and obedient to better counsels should any one show us that the matter had not been properly handled.

About two years after arose one Joachim Westphal, who, so far from being softened to concord by that temperate simplicity of doctrine, seized upon the name of Agreement as a kind of Furies' torch to rekindle the flame. For he avowedly collected from all quarters opinions which he would wish to be thought adverse to each other, that he might thus destroy our Agreement; and showed himself to be inflamed with such a hatred of peace that he vented his peculiar venom against us, for no other reason than that he was annoyed by our thinking and speaking the same thing. . . .

I was forced to repel the perverse attack of this man in a short treatise. As if an inexpiable crime had been committed, he has flamed forth with even greater impetuosity. It has now become necessary for me to repress his insolence. Should I rather inveigh against him vehemently, be pleased to consider in prudence and equity what provocation he has given me. Heresies and heretics, diabolical blasphemies, impious denials of scripture, subversion of all that is sacred, and similar opprobrium, these are the words always to be found on his lips. In short, his book has no other apparent object than to precipitate us by the thunderbolts of anathemas to the lower regions of hell. What was left to me but to apply a hammer to this obstinate nail, and not allow him to have too much freedom in his savage temper? Were there any hope of mollifying men like this, I would not refuse to humble myself, and by supplicating them purchase the peace of the Church. But the lengths to which they go in their violence is notorious to every one concerned.

Tracts II, pp. 246-8

VIII Churches and Martyrs

Calvin believed that reformed churches would be established in response to the Word of God. True believers would gather together into autonomous communities and eventually found their own churches. His task was to offer words of advice, encouragement and occasional reproof to church leaders, laymen and even rulers. He conducted an enormous correspondence across Europe from which one can measure the penetration of Calvinism in various countries.

A England

Calvin's early hopes for the spread of the Word rested upon England. Following the death of Henry VIII in 1547, he hoped that England would proceed without delay to a full Reformation and was encouraged by the early pronouncements of the régime of Protector Somerset during the minority of King Edward VI.[1] Thomas Cranmer, Archbishop of Canterbury, invited many prominent continental divines to London to assist in the godly reformation. Their reports upon the difficulties that they experienced in the task prompted Calvin to write to the Protector in 1549 with some advice.

London became, like Geneva, a refuge for exiles during this period and, by letters-patent of 4 July 1550, a special church was established for those from Flanders, France and Germany. Its first superintendant was John a Lasco (Laski), a Polish nobleman, trained humanist and formerly friend to Erasmus. He had been exiled from his native country in 1539 and established a strong reformed church upon Swiss lines at Emden on the borders of the Netherlands in the Holy Roman Empire. He prudently retired to England after the emperor's victory at

---

[1] A.G. Dickens and D. Carr, *The Reformation in England to the Accession of Elizabeth I* (London, 1967), section VII.

Mühlberg in 1547. A Lasco modelled his London church largely upon Calvin's ordinances for Geneva (*see above* pp. 69–76) but he also devised a number of distinctive features of his own. Ministers and elders were chosen by all the faithful, rather than being co-opted by the ministers or the consistory. Whilst a Lasco's views on the sacraments and predestination did not completely coincide with Calvin's, the two men held each other in high regard. Calvin kept in regular contact with the church in London and, in England, it was seen as a model of the Swiss reform. After it was disbanded by Mary I, individual members of the London congregation were to prove important catalysts for Swiss reform elsewhere in Europe.

140 To Edward Seymour, Earl of Hertford, Duke of Somerset, Protector in England (22 October 1549)

We have every reason to be thankful to our Lord and Father that he has been pleased to employ you in such excellent work as that of setting up the purity and good order of his worship in England by your means, and establishing the doctrine of salvation that it may be faithfully proclaimed to all those who will consent to hear it and that he has granted you such firmness and constancy up to now in spite of so many trials and difficulties. . . .

Calvin warned the Protector not to be dismayed by difficulties.

Seeing that Satan never ceases to raise up new difficulties . . . it would be well to remind you of the sacred history of good King Hezekiah (Chron. 32), namely, that even after he had abolished the superstitions throughout Judea and reformed the state of the Church according to the law of God, he was still pressed by his enemies, so that he appeared to be a lost and ruined man. . . . Thus by this example all faithful princes and governors of countries should be warned that, however earnest they may be in banishing idolatry and in promoting the true worship of God, their faith may yet be tried by different temptations.

Calvin reminded the Protector that his powers came from God and that he should use them to defeat his enemies. He advocated a number of positive measures for the advancement of a godly reformation in England and warned the Protector not to attempt a reformation by halves.

From what I have been given to understand, my Lord, there are two kinds of rebels who have risen against the king and the state. On the

one hand, there are some preposterous individuals who, under cover of
the gospel, are trying to turn everything into confusion. On the other
hand, there are people who persist in the superstition of the Roman
Antichrist.[2] Both alike deserve to be repressed by the sword of authority which is entrusted to you, since they attack not only the king but also
God, who has placed him upon a royal throne and has committed to
you the protection of both his person and his majesty. . . .

It appears to me, my Lord, that there is very little preaching of a
lively kind in the kingdom, but that the majority of clergymen deliver it
by way of reading from a written sermon. I see very clearly the
necessity which constrains you to insist on that; as I understand it,
principally, you have not as many well-trained and trustworthy
ministers of religion as you desire. This deficiency must be remedied as
soon as possible. . . .

There ought to be an explicit summary of the doctrine which all
ought to preach, which all prelates and curates should swear to follow,
and no one should receive any ecclesiastical charge who does not
promise to keep such an agreement. Next, there should be a common
formula of instruction for little children and for ignorant persons,
serving to make them familiar with sound doctrine so that they may be
able to discern the difference between it and the falsehood and corruptions which may be brought forward to oppose it. Believe me, my
Lord, the Church of God will never preserve itself without a
catechism[3], for it is like the seed to keep the good grain from dying
out. . . .

To lop off abuses by halves will by no means restore things to a state
of purity, for then we shall always have a dressed-up Christianity. I say
this because there are some who, under a pretence of moderation, are
in favour of sparing many abuses, without meddling with them at all,
and to whom it appears enough to have rooted out the chief one. But,
on the contrary, we see that the seed of falsehood is fertile, and that only
a single grain is needed to fill the world with it in three days' time, to
such an extent are men addicted and inclined in that direction. . . .

CR XLI, cols. 64–77

The French copy carries no date. The Latin version is dated 22 October 1548,
but this is evidently wrong by a year)

[2] References to the Prayer Book rebellion in Cornwall and Ket's rebellion in Norfolk.
[3] Calvin was apparently unaware of the English catechism which had appeared in
August 1548.

141 Letters patent for the strangers' church in London (24 July 1550)

Considering that it is the duty of a Christian prince to administer the affairs of his kingdom well, to provide for religion and for unhappy exiles, afflicted and banished by reason thereof, we would have you know that, having compassion for the condition of those who have for some considerable time past been domiciled in our kingdom, and come here daily, of our special grace, . . . we will and ordain that henceforth they may have in our city of London a church, to be called the church of our Lord Jesus Christ, where the assembly of the Germans and other strangers can meet and worship for the purpose of having the gospel purely interpreted by the ministers of their church and the sacraments administered according to the Word of God and the apostolic ordinance. . . .

A-N. Schmidt, *Lettres Anglaises (1548–1561)* (Paris, 1959), pp. 92–3

142 To Edward VI, King of England, January 1551

Calvin frequently dedicated printed commentaries on scripture to rulers in the hope that the evangelism inspired by the Word of God properly expounded would bear fruit for reformed Churches. Among the earliest of these dedications was that of the *Book of Isaiah* and the *General Epistles* to Edward VI in January 1551. Calvin forwarded a copy of the books via a minister (Nicholas des Gallars – *see below* p. 170) and included a letter of exhortation to the young king.

As regards a general Reformation, it is not yet so well established as it would be wise to look upon it as achieved. In fact, it would be very difficult to purge in a day such an abyss of superstition as there is to be found in the papacy. Its roots lie too deep and are too extensive to uproot quickly. But no matter what difficulties or delays there may be, the excellence of the task makes it worth unwearied pursuit. . . .

Further, in as much as the schools contain the seeds of the ministry, there is every necessity to keep them pure and thoroughly free from all evil weeds. I speak thus, Sire, because in your universities, it is said that there are many young people supported on college bursaries who, instead of giving good hopes of service in the Church, show, rather, signs of wanting to deny its existence and ruin it, their opposition to the true religion being undisguised. Wherefore, Sire, I beseech you once more, in the name of God, that you may be pleased to take this in hand so that property which ought to be held as sacred is not converted to profane uses in order to nourish venemous reptiles. . . .

CR XLII, cols. 38–41

B Calvin and the Marian Exiles

With Mary Tudor's accession in England in July 1553 the strangers' church was quickly disbanded and, with numerous refugees of conscience, the congregation left for northern Germany, Switzerland and Scandinavia. One group established itself at Wesel, a small town in northern Germany. They soon found the Lutheran inhabitants somewhat intolerant of their Calvinist practices. Calvin's advice to them was to accept with patience and resignation the position God had granted to them but, in 1557, most of the refugees moved to Frankfurt. There, many other refugees had already installed themselves and persuaded the city authorities to grant them permission to congregate as a separate church in March 1554. Calvin was delighted by this news and dedicated his commentary on the *Harmony of the Gospels* to Frankfurt's magistrates in 1555. John Laski also encountered Lutheran opposition when he landed in Norway and again in Emden. He, too, eventually arrived in Frankfurt to become superintendant of the foreigners' church. The tense frustrations and boredom of exile led to numerous squabbles and dissensions. There were disputes amongst the English over the use of the English Prayer Book of 1552 as against a re-written one on fully Calvinist lines[4], whilst the French refugees deposed their minister, Valeran Poulain. Calvin warned the Frankfurt foreigners' church of its 'excessive rigour' and subsequently took the unusual step of journeying to the city in August 1556 to try to heal the various divisions.

143   Ministers of Geneva to the brethren in Wesel (13 March 1554)

We must praise God because, from the troubles which now disturb the

---

[4] Dickens and Carr, *Reformation in England*, pp. 154–7.

peace of the world, he has granted you a place of refuge in which you are at liberty to assemble in his name, to exercise yourselves in the hearing of his Word, to call upon him with one accord, and to make a pure confession of your faith. This is no slight favour when the world is turned upside down. It remains for you to profit by it and prove yourselves so much the more zealous in glorifying him who has bestowed upon you so liberal a gift that it might multiply. As to the form to be observed in receiving the sacraments, it is not without reason that you entertain doubts and scruples, for nothing is better than to keep to that simplicity which comes from the Son of God, whose ordinance ought to be our only rule and to which the apostles also conformed. Indeed the moment we deviate from it (even by a small amount) our human innovation cannot help but be corrupt. But it seems to us that your position is different from that of the ministers and vast majority of the people there. . . . As private individuals, not only may you lawfully support, but, what is more, you ought to suffer, such abuses as it is not in your power to correct. We do not think lighted candles or figured bread[5] used in the celebration of the Eucharist to be such matters of indifference that we would willingly accept their introduction here or approve of them ourselves; but we do not object to their being tolerated where they have been already established and where we have no authority to oppose them. If we were asked to receive such ceremonies, we should hold ourselves bound to accept them, according to the position in which God has placed us, admitting of no compromise in resisting their introduction and in maintaining constantly the purity which the Church already possessed. But should our lot be cast in some place where a different custom prevailed, there is not one of us who, for the sake of a candle or a chasuble, would separate himself from the body of the Church and so deprive himself of the use of the sacraments.

CR XLIII, cols. 78–80

144   Calvin to the church at Frankfurt (22 December 1555)

Beloved Brethren [French exiles in Frankfurt],
      . . . Your attention has been directed to some faults which have been found in our brother, Master Valeran, your pastor. A satisfactory remedy for them has been found and you have every reason to be

---

[5] I.e. Wafers used at the Eucharist with images impressed on them.

satisfied and to accept his discipline. Now, as I understand it, there is a new difference of opinion to be sorted out. Some are inclined not to recognize him as their minister until he has given in his resignation and a new election has been undertaken. For my part, I am obliged to declare that those who insist on such matters have not given them sufficient thought and show an excessive rigour which is little calculated to bring benefit to the church.

CR XLIII, cols. 895–8

24 June 1556
Your letters, telling me that tranquillity is now restored to your church, would have brought me greater pleasure if there were not a rumour widely spread abroad that nothing has changed for the better and that disputes prevail as much as they ever did. . . . I entreat you to preserve as much moderation as possible and not to exasperate those who are already much irritated. I say this with good cause for I wish (and this, frankly, is a commonly-held opinion) you had not acted so rigorously towards those who disapproved of the election that you have made [of a new minister]. . . . I do not want to intrude upon the responsibility of others and I well know the danger that results from a church's undertaking to absolve those who have been condemned by another. I merely tell you what other people will think of you.

CR XLIV, cols. 210–13

C Poland

During the reign of the last of the Jagiellon dynasty, Sigismund Augustus (r. 1548–72), the reformed churches took advantage of his tolerant and enlightened *régime*. Lutheranism spread from Prussia to Great Poland.[6] The Bohemian Brethren gained a following for their crypto-Calvinist views in both Great and Little Poland. The Swiss, or evangelical, Church also established a presence in Little Poland and united with the Bohemian Brethren after its first synod in 1550. Calvin wrote to Sigismund in 1549 and dedicated to him his commentary on

---

[6] Area around Poznan, later called south Prussia. Little Poland was to the south-west, around Krakow, and was later called West Galicia.

the *Epistle to the Hebrews*. Four years later the king sent his personal
envoy, Lismanini (a native of Corfu and a former Provincial of the
Franciscan Order), to survey the Reformation in other parts of
Europe. Calvin welcomed Lismanini to Geneva and, with his encour-
agement, wrote to the king and other important nobles. Amongst the
latter was Nicholas Radziwiłł, whose influence on Sigismund was
considerable and who became famous for producing the first Polish
Bible (the Radziwiłł, or Brest, Bible). In 1556 Calvin was invited to
Poland to advise a diet on the country's Reformation, but the letter was
delayed and Calvin eventually replied by declining the offer. John a
Lasco, however, returned to his native country and, although King
Sigismund refused to undertake a national Reformation, a Lasco spent
the last three years of his life, from 1557 to 1560, in an evangelical
campaign to create a proper evangelical Church in Poland. Calvin
gave him moral encouragement but, after a Lasco's death, it became
clear that Calvinism would remain a small religious minority among
many other denominations in Poland, so long as its religious pluralism
survived.

145   To Sigismund Augustus (December 1554)

. . . Remember, then, most excellent king that a light has been kindled
divinely for the whole of Poland which cannot be overshadowed for
ever without incurring serious blame.

Let this, therefore, be your primary aim, your principal concern: to
assemble the powers subject to you, and call them from the shameful
dissoluteness of popery to the obedience of Christ. Let that heroic
virtue which has lain numb for too long within you at last break forth
and give a memorable proof of its existence on this noble objective. I
am aware that the undertaking is immense and that the difficulties that
threaten it are large and formidable. . . . But when the battle is for the
glory of God in the kingdom of Christ, for the purity of religious worship, for the salvation of the human race, such is the excellence of the
cause that it should outweigh all vexations by its glory and easily overcome all obstacles. . . .

Wherefore, most excellent king, however much the papistical clergy
prate about the divine right of the priesthood, let not their futile drivel
prevent your majesty from attempting . . . the noblest of all works.
. . . This seems to be the proper and advantageous method of
proceeding. Because wolves now occupy the shepherd's place, and

because it might be thought too abrupt a change if ministers, appointed by royal authority alone, could furnish no other authority than yours for their vocation, the method I would propose is this: that your majesty should, for the moment, institute teachers to spread abroad the seeds of the gospel, and their charge should be provisional and last only so long as things remain in their present precarious and unsettled state. For it is not possible that the government of a Church can be changed all at once. But this prelude, or beginning, which I have outlined, would provide a convenient transition for the renovation of the Church. This would not, in fact, be a reformation of it, but only a preliminary step. Things would come to fruition, and by royal authority and in the assembly of the diet a more definite manner of ordaining pastors would be arrived at for the future.

CR XLIII, cols. 330–5

146   To Nicolas Radziwiłł (13 February 1555)

To the Most Illustrious Prince Nicolas Radziwiłł, duke of Olika, Niessen, count of Vilna, grand duke of Lithuania etc.

Whilst it is my wish that the kingdom of Christ should flourish everywhere, yet, at the present time, Poland occupies my thoughts with a special anxiety. For, from the moment that the light of a purer doctrine began to dawn upon it, this happy beginning has, at the same time, inflamed my desire with hopes of even better progress. . . . Since you are naturally inclined to protect pure piety; and since, with heroic greatness of mind, you show your sincerity and faith in this task, this courage of yours justly encourages me to give you thanks and enables me to have greater confidence. For I do not simply ask you to continue to be as you have been in the past, but that, in competition with what you have done in the past, you should reach out for the noblest victory of all . . . the heavenly reign of God on earth.

CR XLIII, col. 428

147   To the nobles of Poland (8 March 1557)

Well-born and noble Seigneurs,
   . . . Though it was easy to understand from your letter that you would be pleased to see me come [to Poland], yet my departure from

this church would bring considerable disadvantages to it. My concern was that my haste to come to assist you before the time was appropriate, might be construed here as inconsiderate and excessive in zeal. . . . At present, by the blessing of God, you have it in your power to profit by the labours of that most excellent and faithful minister in Christ, John Laski, and I do not see so great a necessity for my being with you. For, although I am confident that he would willingly make me a partner to his labours, and whilst it would be the greatest pleasure to me to co-operate with him to your advantage, I do not think that you would want me, unless absolute necessity demanded it, to be torn away from the place where I am usefully employed.

CR XLIV, cols. 419–21

D France

Calvin's greatest impact was naturally in French-speaking lands and his greatest concern was the progress of the Reformation in the kingdom of France. Towards the end of his reign Francis I's policy towards heresy hardened. The distinction between 'Lutherans' and 'Sacramentarians' became blurred in public pronouncements, and a connection between 'heresy' and 'disorder' was established so that in an edict of June 1539 the investigation, torture and punishment of heretics liable to commit a breach of the peace were handed over to the royal courts. In April 1545 the king sent out special judicial commissioners from the *parlement* of Paris to find heretic conventicles, while the *parlement* at Aix brutally suppressed the localized remnants of the late-medieval heretics, the Waldensians (*see above* p. 122). Meanwhile, the first Calvinist community in France was founded at Meaux, the cradle of the French Reformation.

The reign of Francis I's son, Henry II, opened in 1547 with a redoubling of the severity of persecution. Calvin's response was to address an open letter to the faithful, entreating them to courage and resilience. The letter suggests that Calvin was actively in contact with numerous conventicles in France about a decade before the fully fledged Calvinist churches were established in France in the 1550s. Because of the severe persecution all Calvin's letters to France were clandestine. They rarely stated their precise destination and, to lessen the risks of detection,

Calvin used a variety of assumed names, of which the most common in French was Charles d'Espeville.

The edict of Châteaubriant of 27 June 1551 has been described as 'a true code of persecution'. It was exhaustive and comprehensive in its detail and scope. It went far beyond the attempt to limit disorders inherent in 'heresy' and aimed to eliminate Protestantism in France. Calvin's legal background made him keenly aware of the exceptional nature of the edict in the context of French law. Many died for their faith as a result. Their sufferings were recorded with care and loving detail in the famous martyrology of Jean Crespin. Crespin (c. 1520–72) was a lawyer from Arras in Artois. He was suspected for his religious beliefs in 1545 and fled to Paris where he spent three years before leaving for Geneva with his friend Theodore Beza. In due course he established himself as a printer. The *Livre des Martyrs* first appeared as a slim volume in 1554 and was expanded in successive editions in 1556 and 1559 until the definitive edition in 1609. By making readers aware of the courage and endurance of those who suffered for the faith Crespin's work was extremely important in helping morale amongst Calvinists in France. It enabled Calvinists to lay claim to the pure traditions of the early Christian Church, which had also suffered from persecution at its birth.

One of those who died at the stake, and whose martyrdom was recorded by Crespin, was Richard Le Fèvre. He was a goldsmith from Rouen who had been converted to Protestantism when on a visit to London. He later visited Geneva in 1544. He was then captured in Rouen and, while he awaited trial before the *parlement* in the city, Calvin managed to smuggle a letter to him, which Crespin reproduced. Le Fèvre subsequently escaped from custody while he was being transferred from Rouen to Paris, where his case was to be heard on appeal. He was recaptured two years later in Grenoble and burnt at the stake for heresy on 7 June 1554. In May 1554 he wrote his last letter to Calvin from the prison in Lyons.

Amongst the many cases of martyrdom which occurred in the 1550s, the case of the 'five scholars' of Lyons disturbed Calvin deeply. They were five Frenchmen from the Midi who had studied theology at Lausanne college, may have been ordained, and were on their way back to the south-west of France when they were betrayed by a fellow-traveller, imprisoned and burnt at the stake in Lyons on 16 May 1553. Calvin organized diplomatic pressure to be placed on the French king by German Protestant princes (with whom Henry II had an alliance),

and also wrote to the 'five scholars' in prison. Crespin printed one of
these letters, written in December 1552.

148   To the faithful in France (24 July 1547)

Very dear lords and brethren,

. . . I entreat you, my dear brethren, to hold steady upon your
course and let no fear upset you even though the dangers are more
evident now than ever before. May the trust which God commands us
to have in his grace and his strength always be an impregnable fortress
for you; and to keep you assured of his assistance you should be careful
to walk in his fear although, even when our whole effort has been to
serve him, we must always return to this conclusion, that we should ask
his pardon for our faults. Moreover, you know well by experience how
feeble we are, so be always diligent and continue the order that you
have established of prayer and hearing the holy Word, to discipline and
strengthen yourselves more and more. Let nothing turn you aside,
even though many pretty things will be found to distract you. I am sure
that it would be much better if all those who desire to know God should
assemble together so that each one acted as a kind of clarion call to the
others. And yet it is much better to have travelled half the way, as you
have, than not to have set out at all. Do not retreat, but go forward and
profit and make use of what God gives you – edifying one another and
all the poor and ignorant folk in general by your good lives so that, by
your example, the wicked will be put to confusion. . . . [signed]
Charles d'Espeville

CR XL, cols. 562–3

149   Reactions to the Edict of Châteaubriant (15 October 1551)

Calvin to Bullinger, 15 October 1551

. . . Some frightful laws have been published by which a permanent
institution in the kingdom is torn away so that new ways of expressing
hatred towards the pious ones are manifested. What has hitherto been
granted to sorcerers, forgers and thieves, and is still there, namely, that
they have a right of appeal to a sovereign court, is now taken away from
Christians, whom ordinary magistrates, without any appeal, may
order to be delivered to the flames forthwith. It is forbidden for relatives of those whose lives are thus at risk to venture to protest on pain of

being treated as accessories to heresy. In order to keep the flames well fanned, one third of their goods is allotted to informers. If the judges consider any one negligent, he suffers a penalty. Should the judgement appear too lenient, the judge is liable to a reprimand.

The Lord Chancellor is to take care not to admit any person to a public office who may, at any time, have fallen under the slightest suspicion with the result that no one can become a judge who is not hostile to Christ. Any one who hopes for an appointment to public service has to produce a sheaf of testimonials proving him an obedient son of the Church of Rome. A penalty is imposed on the sponsors of any one who gains an office by deception. There is a punishment for cities which elect town councillors that are in the slightest degree suspected of Lutheranism. The law requires the sovereign courts to ensure that any attorneys who are known to favour our teaching should clear themselves upon oath. Every one is required to worship the bread-God by the usual earnest genuflections.

Parishes are required to read the Sorbonne articles[7] to the people every Sunday for their benefit so that a solemn abnegation of Christ may resound throughout the land. The goods of all those who come as exiles to us are confiscated to the treasury even if they were sold or disposed of in any way before they left unless the judges allow it to have been properly and deliberately sold previously. Geneva is mentioned more than 10 times, always with a mark of infamy attached to it. A similar note is affixed to all places which have completely separated from the see of Rome. This ferocity is necessary in order that the direst confusion may follow. The flames are already kindled everywhere, and all the highways are guarded lest any one should seek asylum here. . . . How ominous! The sword is whetted for our throats.

CR XLII, cols. 186–7

150   Calvin to Richard Le Fèvre (19 January 1551)

My dear brother,
    As God has called you to give testimony to his gospel, never doubt that he will strengthen you in the might of his Spirit; and that, as he has already begun, so he must needs perfect his work, manifesting his

---

[7] 25 articles of faith drawn up by the Sorbonne in Paris on 10 March 1543 and ratified by the king on 23 July 1543 as the official religion of France.

victory against his enemies in you. It is true that the triumphs of Jesus Christ are despised by the world; for while we are being persecuted, the wicked glorify themselves in their pride. They will be confounded by the glory of that truth which God has put into our mouths, our hearts will be strengthened to obtain the victory over Satan and all his supporters, whilst looking for the day when the glory of God shall fully be revealed to the confusion of the wicked and the unbelievers. All that you have felt and experienced until now of the abounding goodness of God ought to confirm you in the assured hope that he will not fail you in the future. Meanwhile, pray to him that he will make you understand even better what a treasure there is in the beliefs for which you fight, so that in comparison you may not esteem even your life to be precious.

Richard Le Fèvre to Calvin from the prison at Lyons, 3 May 1554
The present is to let you know that I hope to go and keep Whitsuntide in the kingdom of heaven and to be present at the marriage of the Son of God . . . if I am not sooner called away by this good Lord and Master whose voice I am now ready to obey, when he shall say, 'Come, ye blessed of my Father, possess the kingdom which has been prepared for you before the foundation of the world. . . .'

CR XLII, cols. 18–19; XLIII, col. 129

151   The 'Five Scholars' of Lyons (December 1552)

You know, my brethren, that we must be prepared to be offered as sacrifices to him. You will assuredly suffer harsh treatment so that what was said of Peter may be fulfilled in you: 'You will be taken where you have no wish to go' (John 21, 18). But you know the courage that you must use in your fight; in this way all those who have relied on you will never be taken by surprise and still less be thrown into confusion. So, my brethren, be assured that you will be strengthened in your hour of need by the spirit of our Lord Jesus Christ not to give way under stress of temptation, however severe, any more than he did whose victory was so glorious that it is certain guarantee for us that we shall triumph in the midst of our suffering. Since it pleases him to make use of you until death itself to uphold his cause, he will give you strength to strive constantly and he will not allow one drop of your blood to be without its use.

CR XLII, cols. 423–4

152   Antoine Laborie's interrogation (August–September 1555)

Certain groups of martyrs gained notoriety. Along with the 'Five Scholars' of
Lyons came the 'Five Pastors' of Chambéry. A group of five ministers were on
their way from Geneva to missions in France when they were captured at
Fossigny in Savoy. They were imprisoned, tried and burnt at Chambéry. One
of the five, Antoine Laborie, sent Calvin a vivid account of his courtroom
appearance which was not without its tragi-comic moments and which reveals
in its intimate way the mental world of one of the Calvinist martyrs.

On Friday morning at 7 a.m. [23 August 1555] someone came to fetch
me and take me before their lordships in their chambers. There sitting
in their chairs were the two presidents, nine councillors, the king's
advocate and the clerk. Upon entry, one of them instructed the clerk to
show me a picture with a crucifix painted on it, and ordered me to go
down on my knees before it. I replied, 'For God's sake, may it please
you, I will not bow before any graven image'. Then I was told, 'What
cheek! Do you think the court means you to worship the image and not
ourselves as well? On the contrary, the court commands you to worship
God and honour the magistrate, and to do this you go down on your
knees and swear before your God to tell the truth and answer questions
with respect'. 'Your lordships', I said, 'I wish to worship God and
honour Him and, besides that, to obey the magistrate. I will do as you
command, provided that the picture is removed and not otherwise'.
Then he told the clerk to take it away and ordered me again to go down
on my knees, declaring that the court only wished me to adore God and
show my respect for the magistrate. . . .

   Thus the cause of idolatry was raised before they even asked my
name, and was discussed for quite some time. Afterwards they asked
me my name, date of birth and profession, and I replied truthfully to
them all. The president asked me about my capture and about the law-
suit so far and about our sentence, telling me that the royal prosecutor
had brought the case upon appeal. To this I replied by telling him what
had happened and that, as to the sentence . . . I was ready to receive
patiently all that it pleased God to send me – freedom, death, the
galleys, seeing that it was in His name that I would suffer one or the
other. Upon that, he asked me why I had left my country and gone to
Geneva. I replied to him that it was because of the truth. He then told
me to stand up and afterwards lectured me, using all sorts of entice-
ments, protesting that I could as easily have stayed at home and served
God there as in Geneva, that I had offended the Almighty by leaving
my home and causing a fuss. Passages from holy scripture were even

used against me. At the end of the lecture, he argued that we were all responsible for our own actions, that we had free will, that the Pope (whilst his life was not a perfect one, and he admitted that) was at least a bishop, and that it was wrong to call him Antichrist; that the mass was the Supper and a sacrifice by an action of grace. . . . Upon that, although my flesh was terribly scared, the Lord inspired me to reply, with the reason why I could not with a healthy conscience remain with the papacy, being deprived of the Word and the sacraments. . . .

The ending of our discussion was such that (whether truly or as a ruse I know not) the judge agreed with me that we lacked free will, that we were justified by faith rather than by works, that the mass was stuffed with a myriad of superfluities rendering it worthless; that it could not be a sacrifice for our sins but only an action of grace; that the body of Jesus Christ was not located in the bread, nor the blood in the wine; and that those who worshipped it there were idolatrous. . . . In brief, he accepted nearly everything, so that I was forced to say to him, 'My lord, I wish the Lord had given such grace to every monk in France as he has given to you to be a good theologian; for we would soon come to an agreement. And I can see that I should not be afraid of your condemning me unless you did so against your own conscience. For, if I am a heretic (which I am not), you are also one by your own profession'. Upon that, all the councillors began to laugh, and one of them, the judge who was summing up our case, said, 'You mean you should be a heretic like him, and not him like you'. To this I replied, 'My lord, I do not want to be like him, for perhaps I would be an imposter. At least that is the common and widely held view, and I would prefer that you were all like me'.

The president blushed at this and began to exhort me to make a recantation . . . and seeing that he was not making any headway, had me led away. . . . I was put in a little room apart from my brethren, which was hard for me, for I wanted to inform them of the cunning tricks of the judges. But suddenly I was greatly comforted by the knowledge of the help that the Lord had given me, because of which I began to render him thanks and pray for my brethren who had not yet been called. And seeing that the president had agreed with me, as I have said, I felt an overwhelming desire to speak to him and preach the judgement of God before him. . . . I remained thus, praying and meditating until 2 p.m. when the servant came to tell me that . . . I should go before their lordships and say what I wanted to. Overjoyed by such news, I went before them. . . . Then, raising up my spirit to

God to ask his help, I began by reminding them of their office, and why God had constituted them watchers over his people, and had even called them gods after His own name, and exhorted them to fulfil their duties according to his will. Afterwards, I repeated that I and my brethren were innocent, which they could not be ignorant of, since they had admitted it that morning. . . . And thus they should be in favour of the cause of Jesus Christ since they were judges of Him through us, since we were his adherents, warning them not to commit a sin before the Holy Spirit; upon which I presented the living judgement of God, and finally I told them of the care the Lord took of his own and how he required their sacrifice. In sum, God gave me the grace to be listened to for about an hour without interruption. I told them everything that the Lord gave me to say with the application of passages from scripture. . . . Whilst I spoke they all had their eyes on me and I on them, and I saw some of the younger men had tears in theirs. When I had finished, one of their leaders said that he agreed with what I had said about their office, but that I well knew that God had commanded through Moses that heretics should be punished before any one else and that, whilst some of the things which I had said might have been true, I could not deny that others had offended and scandalized my neighbours, calling the Pope Antichrist and the son of perdition, and the mass the invention of the devil, a monkey trick and a work of every abomination, for which I could not be held innocent, and many other things. I agreed with him that it was necessary to punish heretics, and mentioned to him Servetus, who had been punished in Geneva; but that they should look at it carefully lest they punished Christians and God's children instead of heretics. . . . Finally he repeatedly begged me just to retract before them and then they would let me go, seeing that I could do so much good, and that this retraction would not be dangerous. . . .

On the following Monday, 26 August, we were all led before their lordships, who made a great speech and enjoined upon us to retract. .. . Brother Vernon, by God's grace, replied fully for us all that we would glorify our God and we would return victorious. Since then, all five of us have apparently been condemned to be burnt. We render our thanks to God and await the time. . . .

J. Crespin, *Histoire des martyrs, persecutez et mis à mort* . . . (Geneva, 1619), p. 647

Throughout the 1550s groups of Calvinists in France met secretly, organized themselves into congregations and corresponded with Geneva. Calvin provided advice on how to establish a church and, later on, helped to provide ministers trained in Geneva. The Protestant church in Paris was one of the most important in the country. It was founded in September 1555 by a nobleman called Jean Le Maçon, seigneur de Launoy. Many pastors used assumed names to avoid detection and de Launoy was known as La Rivière for this reason. The early history of the Parisian church – with many other churches in France – was comprehensively related in a work which was later edited and published in Geneva called the *Ecclesiastical History of the Reformed Churches of France* (*Histoire ecclésiastique* . . ., 1580). Inevitably, some reformed congregations in France considered the possibility of armed resistance when faced with sustained persecution. Calvin heard of these discussions at some stage in 1556 and issued an impassioned letter to the church involved (it has been suggested that it was at Angers, although the evidence is inconclusive) not to consider resistance to constituted authority. Calvin was entirely consistent with the views which he held in the *Institutes* (*see above* pp. 63–4). The first national synod of the French churches was held in 1557 in Paris, and 11 churches sent deputies to draw up a confession of faith and a common ecclesiastical discipline. The growth of congregations and regular meetings of churches increased the risks of sectarian riots inspired by fears of traditionally minded Catholics in France's cities and towns. A few days after the news of France's disastrous military defeat at St Quentin, Parisian anger and fear was directed against the Protestants. On 4 September 1557 a night-time meeting of the church in Paris was surprised by students from the nearby *collège* Du Plessis in the rue Saint-Jacques in the Latin quarter. A religious riot ensued in which many Protestants were arrested and badly treated while in prison in the Châtelet, the Paris prison. The riot proved to be the pattern which many similar disturbances would take in the capital, especially during the earlier phases of the civil wars. Calvin sent his condolences to the remnants of the Paris congregation and promised them that nothing was being spared in an effort to help them – a reference to the diplomatic efforts under way with certain German princes to put pressure on their ally, the French king, to show more humanity to the French Protestants. Towards the end of the same year Calvin also attempted to persuade the senior prince of the blood, Antoine de Bourbon, king of Navarre, to speak up for the Protestants at court. In December 1557 he

learnt that the king had accepted reformed preachers to his court at
Nérac in south-western France and had been invited to Paris to attend
an estates-general of the kingdom. Calvin immediately wrote to
persuade the king of Navarre either to make an open profession of faith
or, at least, to work for the relief of persecution of the churches. In fact,
Navarre did not arrive in Paris until the following March and, either
because of ambition or (more probably) because he lacked strong
religious convictions, he did not champion the Protestant cause while
he was there. From then until his death at the siege of Rouen in 1562,
Navarre refused to play the part of leader that some French Protestants
had cast for him.

153   To a French congregation (19 June 1554)

. . . You are also doing well to meet together both to invoke in your
midst the name of God and also to receive such good and holy instruction as God's grace endows upon some to teach the rest. For, given our
manifest frailty, such discipline is necessary to us until we leave this
world. We need to be even more thoroughly fortified when Satan is
making such efforts to destroy our faith.

With the use of the sacraments, you must make sure that you build
only upon firm foundations. When you meet together, every one
amongst you should bring along such talents as those which God has
granted him, and whoever has been more generously endowed can
share his with the rest. Those who are not yet so confident should
modestly and humbly receive what is laid before them. But to teach is a
very different thing from administering the sacraments. For to have a
man who may distribute to you the holy Supper of our Lord Jesus
Christ, first of all he must be elected and chosen by you all in common.
And in order to do this, you must have a certain and established community constituted as a church. You must be resolved on following up
the business and organization of assembling yourselves which you have
already begun. We do not require you to make a public confession of
your faith, for we are well aware of the strict tutelage in which you are
held, and under these circumstances it is quite sufficient that the little
flock should assemble in secret. As a result, it is necessary that you
should agree amongst yourselves to meet both for joint prayers and for
the preaching of the Word, in order to have the form of the church.
This established, when there is some one among you who is fit to be
called to the office of pastor, it will be his duty to administer the

sacraments to you. But take heed that those who come forward with you to receive the sacraments in such purity as God has ordained are not still contaminated with papal superstitions, but that you may, in reality, be separated from anything which is opposed to our Lord Jesus Christ.

CR XLIII, cols. 173–4

154   The church in Paris (September 1555)

The inauguration of this church came about through the agency of a nobleman from Maine, le Sieur de la Ferrière, who had come to Paris with his family so as to escape observation because of his religion. In particular it was because his wife was pregnant and he did not want the child whom God should give him to be baptized with the usual superstitious ceremonial and ritual of the Roman Church. Some time later la Rivière and some others met together on one occasion at the house of the nobleman, in the district known as Préaux Clercs, for prayer and Bible reading. . . . As it happened that the lady had now had her baby, La Ferrière asked the gathering not to allow the child whom God had given him to be deprived of baptism by which Christian children ought to be dedicated to God. So he asked them to select a minister who could undertake the baptism. When the company did not want to agree he pointed out to them that his conscience did not allow him to accept the conglomeration and corruption of baptism into the Church of Rome. It was impossible for him to go to Geneva for this purpose. If the child died without his service he would be extremely sorry and he would appeal to God against them if they would not do what he so rightly asked them in God's name. This event was the occasion for the first meetings of the church of Paris. La Rivière was chosen by the congregation after prayer and fasting, as was appropriate, and taken even more carefully and seriously than usual since it was an innovation there. Then they set up a small establishment as far as their limited numbers would allow by forming a consistory of some elders and deacons to supervise the church, all this following as closely as possible the example set by the primitive Church of apostolic times.

Beza I, p. 98

155   To a French church (19 April 1556)

For the rest, I have heard that some are debating among themselves whether, if an atrocity is committed against them, they would resort to violence rather than allow themselves to be hunted down by brigands. I beseech you, beloved brethren, to abandon any such notions for they will never obtain God's blessing and will never succeed since he disapproves of such things. I well understand what distress you feel, but it is not in my power – nor that of any living creature – to grant you dispensation to act in opposition to the will of God. When you are in trouble for having done nothing except your duty, this consolation will not fail you, that God will look upon you with compassion and come to your aid in some way or another. But if you strive to do more than permitted to you, then not only will your expectations be frustrated, but you will have the bitter remorse of sensing that God is against you. . . . If you are tormented by the unrighteous for having heard the Word of God, withdrawn yourselves from idolatries and confessed the gospel of Christ, at least you shall always have this to support you, that you suffer in a righteous cause, and one in which God has promised that he will stand by you. But he has not armed you to resist those who are established by him to govern.

CR XLIV, cols. 112–13

156   Incident in the rue Saint-Jacques (4 September 1557)

Calvin to the church in Paris, 16 September 1557
Dearly Beloved Seigneurs and Brethren,

I need not dwell at great length on how much the news of your sufferings has pained and saddened us. The intimate bond which binds us all to our common cause is enough to explain our distress. If we had it in our power to show you by our actions the desire we have to lessen your affliction, you would feel it more effectively. But, beyond our prayers on your behalf we cannot do much, though other means of coming to your aid are not neglected by us. We do not know if they will help you, but do not doubt that God has you in mind and that your tears and lamentations will be listened to by him. For if we do not trust to his providence, distress will become an abyss which will swallow us up. We shall be shaken to and fro at every breath of wind; we shall be troubled in our perplexities and led astray in our counsels; in a word, our whole life will be a labyrinth, especially when Satan and his agents have been let loose to torment and molest the poor Church of God.

Among those attacked and imprisoned in the incident were many artisans and women, for the appeal of Calvinism was never restricted to any particular social group. Calvin wrote to the women in prison to remind them that God asked the same sacrifice of them, as of men.

You see that the truth of God, wherever it is found, is the object of their hatred. It is no less detestable to them in men than in women, in the learned than in the ignorant, in the rich than in the poor, in the great than in the small. If they use the excuse of sex or social status to fall more furiously upon us (and we see how they deride women and poor artisans, as if they had not the right to speak of God and learn the way of salvation), then you will recognize that such conduct is a testimony against them and to their utter ruin. But since it has pleased God to call you as well as men (for the sex does not matter to him), it is important that you do your duty and give him the glory according to the measure of grace which he has dealt out to you.

CR XLIV, cols. 629-30

157 To Antoine de Bourbon, King of Navarre (14 December 1557)

. . . Sire, the sighs and groans of so many true believers deserve your attention. You should be courageous and come to their aid, procuring their relief so far as it is in your power to do so. At present no more fitting moment could be found than in this assembly of the estates. Probably in their discussions of public administration, they will touch upon the question of religion. Many will think it repugnant, I know, that you should try to sustain the cause of Jesus Christ. But if you, Sire, who ought to be the instrument of all the children of God, keep silent, who else will be bold enough to open his mouth and say a word? Do not wait until God sends you a messenger from heaven, but take it for granted that, in calling you to such an assembly and with such a rank as yours, you are the witness and advocate of his cause. . . . If the circumstances do not allow you to stand up for what is right with entire freedom and condemn what is evil, the least that you can do is to ask for an investigation so that many poor people are not condemned without good reason. At the same time it would be appropriate for you to demonstrate by well-chosen arguments that it is not for the tranquillity and advantage of the kingdom to proceed by violent means, inasmuch as the fires of persecution do but increase the numbers of the persecuted, so that the blood of martyrs becomes the seed of the Church.

CR XLIV, cols. 732-3

IX   The Last Years (1559–1564)

A Calvin and John Knox

John Knox (1505–72) was, more than any other individual, responsible for the Calvinist reformation in Scotland. A scholar and divine, he arrived as an exile in Geneva in April 1555. After the lawlessness and violence of Scotland and the bitter divisions of the Protestant refugees in Frankfurt, Knox found in Geneva a city of Protestant idealists like himself and he promptly became a Calvinist. During his exile he became more involved with English exiles and, in December 1556, he was instituted the minister to their congregation in Geneva. This led him to write his famous pamphlet, the *First Blast of the Trumpet against the Monstrous Regiment of Women* which was published in Geneva in the spring of 1558 without either Calvin's knowledge, or the city's permission or cognisance. It advanced the view that female rulers were against the law of God and contrary to the laws of nature. Most of the pamphlet was aimed at the hated Mary Tudor, but some parts of the work were addressed against all female rulers. A few months later Knox followed this with other works, notably his *Letter to the commonalty of Scotland* (dated 14 July 1558), in which he admitted the authorship of the *First Trumpet* and gave a short synopsis for its sequel which advocated the legality of political revolution for religious ends. Both these works were deeply embarrassing to Calvin and the Genevan authorities. After having read the *First Trumpet Blast*, Calvin took immediate steps to ban the sale of the book in Geneva. He also wrote to various English exiles to disassociate himself from Knox's opinions. The damage in England, however, was great. Elizabeth I became queen in November 1558 and Calvin promptly dedicated his *Commentary on Isaiah* to her. In return, he received a cool letter from her secretary, William Cecil, protesting at Knox's publications in Geneva and holding Calvin responsible. Calvin hastened to explain his ignorance of the works and his distaste for them but the impression that

Geneva and political revolution were associated was not removed. Beza reported in 1566 that it explained part of Elizabeth's subsequent hostility towards Calvinism.

Meanwhile, John Knox returned to Scotland, having been persuaded to do so by Calvin and other ministers in Geneva. He arrived at Leith in May 1559 and played a major part in the turbulent politics of the Scottish Reformation over the following decade. In August 1560 the Scottish parliament abolished papal jurisdiction within Scotland and in the same year the *First Confession of Faith* was produced which indicated how thoroughly Calvinist the Scots Kirk had become. Few letters between Calvin and Knox survive from these years. Those which remain make it clear that Calvin was concerned at the abrasive style and uncompromising attitudes of Knox, afraid perhaps of the risks of a civil war such as the one taking place in France at the same moment.

158 Preface to *The First Blast of the Trumpet . . .* (1558)

Wonder it is, that amongst so many pregnant wits as the Isle of Great Britanny hath produced, so many godly and zealous preachers as England did some time nourish, and amongst so many learned, and men of grave judgement, as this day by Jezebel are exiled, none is found so stout of courage, so faithful to God, nor loving to their native country, that they dare admonish the inhabitants of that isle, how abominable before God is the empire or rule of a wicked woman, yea, of a traitress and bastard; and what may a people or nation, left destitute of a lawful head, do by the authority of God's Word in electing and appointing common rulers and magistrates.

John Knox, *Works* IV, p. 363

159 *Letter to the Commonalty of Scotland . . .* (14 July 1558)

The last section of the treatise was a short note containing a note by Knox that admitted that he was the author of *The First Blast of the Trumpet* and which gave a short summary of four propositions which would appear in its sequel, *The Second Blast of the Trumpet.*

1. It is not birth only, nor propinquity of blood, that maketh a king lawfully to reign above a people professing Christ Jesus and His eternal verity, but in his election must the ordinance which God hath

established in the election of inferior judges be observed.

2. No manifest idolater nor notorious transgressor of God's holy
precepts ought to be promoted to any public regiment, honour or
dignity in any realm, province or city that hath subjected the self to
Christ Jesus and to His blessed Evangel.

3. Neither can oath nor promise bind any such people to obey and
maintain tyrants against God and against His truth known.

4. But if either rashly they have promoted any manifest wicked
person, or yet ignorantly have chosen such a one as after declareth
himself unworthy of regiment above the people of God (and such be all
idolaters and cruel persecutors) most justly may the same men depose
and punish him that unadvisedly before they did nominate, appoint
and elect.

John Knox, Works IV, pp. 539–40

160   To William Cecil (undated – c. March 1559)

The messenger to whom I gave my commentaries on Isaiah to be
offered to the queen brought me back word that my homage was rather
distasteful to her majesty because she was offended with me on account
of certain writings that have been published in this city. . . . Now
though just causes prevent me from providing a long justification of
myself, I have thought it proper to present you with the main facts of
the case lest my silence should be construed in some sense as indicating
a guilty conscience.

Two years ago John Knox asked me in the course of a private talk for
my opinion upon female government. I answered frankly that because
it was a deviation from the primitive and established order of nature, it
ought to be held as a judgement on man for his deriliction of his rights
just like slavery; that, nevertheless, certain women had sometimes
been so gifted that the singular blessing of God was conspicuous in
them, and made it manifest that they had been exalted by the providence of God, either because he willed by such examples to condemn the
indolence of men, or thus to display more clearly his glory. I here gave
the examples of Huldah and Deborah. I also added that God promised
by the mouth of Isaiah that queens should be the nursing mothers of the
Church, which clearly distinguished such persons from private
women. Finally I added in conclusion that since by custom, common
consent and long-established practice it had been admitted that

kingdoms and principalities might be transmitted hereditarily to
women, the question was immaterial and unseemly in itself because in
my judgement it is not permitted to unseat governments that have been
set up by the peculiar providence of God. Of the book I had not the
slightest knowledge and it had been published a whole year before I
knew of its existence.

Informed of it by some people, I made it clear and unequivocal that
the public was not to be teased with paradoxes of that kind. But because
the remedy did not depend on me I decided that an evil which I could
not suppress had better be quietly passed over rather than publicly
canvassed. . . . Of the contents of the work I am ignorant. . . . If my
sloth is offensive, I think I had reason to fear that, if there had been a
public trial, an unfortunate crowd of exiles would, through the
inconsiderate vanity of one man, have been driven from this city and
also from almost every part of the world.

CR XLV, cols. 490-1

161 John Knox's return to Scotland

At the same tyme [1558] some of the Nobilitie direct thare literis to call
JOHN KNOX from Geneva, for thare conforte, and for the conforte of
thare brethrein the preachearis, and otheris that then couragiouslye
faught against the ennemyes of Goddis trewth. The tenour of thare
lettre is this:

Grace, Mercy and Peace, for Salutatioun Etc., Deirlie beloved in
the Lord, the Faithfull that ar of your acquentance in thir partes
(thankis be unto God) ar stedfast in the beleve whareinto ye left thame,
and hes ane godly thrist and desyre, day by day, of your presence
agane; quhilk, gif the Spreat of God will sua move and permitt tyme
unto yow, we will hartly desyre yow, in the name of the Lord, that ye
will returne agane in thir partes, whare ye shall fynd all faithfull that ye
left behynd yow, not only glaid to hear your doctrin but wilbe reddy to
jeopard lyffis and goodis in the forward setting of the glorie of God, as
he will permitt tyme[1], . . .

These letteris war delivered to the said Johne in Geneva. . . . Which
receaved, and advised upoun, he took consultatioun alsweall with his

[1] Letter despatched on 10 March 1557 and signed by the earls of Glencairn and
Argyle, John Erskine earl of Mar, and James Stewart earl of Moray, illegitimate son of
James V of Scotland.

awin church as with that notable servand of God Johne Calvin, and
with other godlie ministers, who all with one consent, said, 'That he
could nott refuise that Vocatioun, onless he wald declair him self
rebellious unto his God, and unmercyfull to his contrie'.

John Knox, History of the Reformation in
Scotland, in Works I, pp. 267–8

162   First Confession of Faith (1560)

We believe in one Church, that is to say, one company and multitude
of men chosen of God who rightly worship him by true faith in Christ
Jesus who is the only head of the same Church. . . . And therefore we
utterly abhor the blasphemy of them that affirm that men who live
according to equity and justice shall be saved whatever religion they
have professed. The marks of the true Church of God we believe,
confess and swear to be, first, the true preaching of the Word of God, in
which God has revealed himself unto us as the writings of the prophets
and apostles do declare. Secondly the right administration of the
sacraments of Christ Jesus, which may be annexed unto the word and
promise of God to seal and confirm the same in our hearts. Last,
ecclesiastical discipline uprightly administered, as God's Word
prescribes, whereby vice is repressed and virtue nourished.

John Knox, Works II, pp. 93–5

163   Calvin to John Knox (23 April 1561)

. . . I am delighted, as you can easily imagine, that the gospel has made
such rapid and easy progress among you. That violent opposition
should have been stirred up against you is nothing new. But the power
of God is more clearly displayed in this, for no attacks either from
Satan or from the ungodly have hitherto prevented you from
advancing with triumph directly on your path, though you could never
have been equal to the task of resisting them unless He who is superior
to all the world had held out to you from heaven a helping hand. With
regard to ceremonies, I trust that you will moderate your rigorous
attitude, even if you cause displeasure to many. It is, of course, your
duty to see that the Church is purged of all the abuses which flow from
error and superstition. . . . But you are well aware that certain things

should be tolerated as exceptions even if you do not quite approve of
them. I am deeply disturbed, as you may well believe, that the nobles of
your nation are split into factions. . . . God is to be entreated to heal
this evil as well.

CR XLVI, cols. 434–5

B Calvin and the Coming of Civil War in France

Sectarian strife, political division and eventual civil war in France
overshadowed the last five years of Calvin's life. In April 1559 the
treaty of Cateau-Cambrésis ended the long series of wars fought by the
Valois kings of France against the Habsburgs. It restored the duchy of
Savoy from French occupation to Emanuele Philibert, duke of Savoy,
an inveterate enemy to Geneva and the two powers even discussed the
possibility of eliminating Geneva as an independent Protestant city by
means of a joint invasion. In fact, peace had come to France because of
royal bankruptcy and to this was added the political tensions resulting
from Henry II's death in July 1559 and the accession of a 15-year-old
king, Francis II, controlled by the ultra-Catholic Guise faction.

Calvin predicted some kind of sectarian disorder in France as early
as October 1559 at precisely the moment when he first heard rumours
of a possible conspiracy in which various members of the lesser nobility
planned to execute a bloodless *coup d'état*, imprison the Guises and
replace them at court with Louis de Bourbon, prince of Condé, brother
to the king of Navarre and second prince of the blood. The conspiracy
miscarried outside Amboise in March 1560, and its military leader,
Jean du Barry, seigneur de La Renaudie (sometimes known as La
Forest), a gentleman from the Périgord, was captured with his
secretary on 18 March in the forest of Châteaurenault, not far from
Amboise.

From the testimony of those captured, the prince of Condé and
Gaspard de Coligny, one of the Constable de Montmorency's nephews
and a well-known Protestant, were implicated in the conspiracy. A
year later, and partly in order to defend the Protestants from the charge
of being rebellious, Calvin wrote for Coligny an account of his involvement in the affair. He described how, in late September or early
October 1559, a 'certain person' came to Geneva with a scheme to

replace the Guises with a prince of the blood, but not necessarily Navarre. This was the minister of the church in Paris, Antoine de la Roche-Chandieu. He probably knew something of the conspiracy that was being put together without in any way being an intimate client of the prince of Condé or the noblemen who eventually executed the plot. Calvin replied that the conspiracy was clearly rebellion and unwarranted unless it was on behalf of the first prince of the blood, supported by the senior judges in the *parlement* and executed without loss of blood. In effect, he offered it no encouragement.

Then, perhaps in December, Calvin met in Geneva La Renaudie himself who was trying to raise men, troops and support amongst the French exiles. Calvin made his own disapproval evident, but La Renaudie continued to use Calvin's name and that of Coligny to persuade people to join the plot. In retrospect, it appears as though Calvin was remarkably successful in ensuring that no minister and only a handful of French Protestant churches offered their support to the coup. It was, however, increasingly unrealistic of him to expect French Protestants to suffer and to die for a duty of obedience when, despite Protestant apologies, they were widely believed in the wake of the failed conspiracy to have been responsible for fomenting rebellion.

164   To Peter Martyr (4 October 1559)

Meanwhile, everything is tending towards a horrible butchery because those who have professed themselves the disciples of Christ and have frequented secret assemblies [in] France are denounced as apostates.

CR XLV, col. 653

165   To Bullinger (5 October 1559)

In Paris the cruelty of the enemies of the gospel rages more furiously than it appears hitherto to have done. Commissioners have orders to go over the whole city and enquire from house to house in what manner each person conducts himself and whether he goes to mass on all the feast days. They not only make their way into bed-chambers, but rummage through beds, chests, coffers, so that they may forthwith drag to prison those in whose possession a suspected book is discovered. They turn all the household furniture upside down, and menace the heads of households with punishment if they are found to have sheltered a Lutheran in their home. They strictly enjoin all neighbours to spy on one another under severe penalties for negligence. Under this pretext, several houses have been pillaged. Lately, an event took place which will inflame their rage. Some 15 nobles were dining together in an inn. In a flash, the commissioners went to work. The beadles broke down the windows. As the intrusion seemed hostile and seditious, these nobles drew their swords and began to repel force with force. One of the beadles was killed and a good many others were wounded. Thus, unless God provides us with a remedy in time, there will be no end to the bloodshed.

CR XLV, cols. 655–6

166   To Gaspard de Coligny (16 April 1561)

Seven or eight months before the event [the Conspiracy of Amboise], a certain person on behalf of some others consulted me as to whether it was not lawful to resist the tyranny by which the children of God were then oppressed, and what means might be employed for that purpose. As I perceived that opinions of this sort were becoming very wide-spread, I gave him a forthright answer that he should abandon all thoughts of this kind, and I then strove to demonstrate to him that he had no warrant for such conduct according to God; and that, even according to the world, such measures were light-headed, frivolous and could not succeed. He was at no loss for an answer and one with even a certain plausibility.

For, he said, it was a question, not of attacking the king or his authority, but only of establishing a government according to the laws of the country during the minority of the king. Meanwhile, the cries of alarm about the inhumanity used to abolish the reformed religion were so great that, hour by hour, they expected a horrible massacre to exterminate all the poor brethren. I replied simply to such objections by stating that if a single drop of blood were to be spilled, rivers of blood would flow across Europe; that for this reason it would be better that we should perish a hundred times than expose Christianity and the gospel to such opprobrium. I admitted, it is true, that if the princes of the blood demanded to be maintained in their rights for the common good, and if the courts of *parlement* joined them in their quarrel, then it would be lawful for all good subjects to lend them armed assistance. The man afterwards asked me whether we were not justified in supporting one of the princes of the blood, even if he were not the first in rank, if he decided to take such a step. I replied to this proposition with the answer no. In short, I adopted so negative a tone in condemning all his proposals that I was convinced that he had completely abandoned them. And that is why I did not breathe a syllable on the subject because it would only have been breeding disturbance to no good purpose.

Some time after that, I was very much astonished when La Renaudie, upon his arrival from Paris, told me that he had been entrusted with the direction of such an enterprise, demonstrating the value of his cause with all the sophisms he could muster. What is more, Sire, I must state that he represented you as mixed up in the business. Now, having always known him as a person puffed up with vanity and self-conceit, I rejected all his propositions so that he could never wring from me the slightest token of consent for them; on the contrary, I strove to turn him aside from these follies by many reasons which it would be too tedious to enumerate. Seeing himself thus frustrated in his expectations, he plotted in secret both to seduce those whom he knew to have but little judgement and also to empty the purses of those who would not have wanted to march with him. All this was done in small groups and under an oath not to disclose anything that was going on. Now there was one who was not so keen to open his wallet and he spoke to Master Pierre Viret [see above, p. 46] about it and revealed that La Renaudie had solicited a contribution from him and made him swear not to say a word about it especially to me because I was unwilling that it should be known that I had given my consent to the enterprise. Master Pierre Viret, without a moment's hesitation, came to me, as in duty bound, and forthwith I begged Master Beza to send for the man. I also called in some witnesses, in whose name I sharply rebuked him for having made use of my name under false pretences. He protested and swore that he had done no such thing, confessing of his own accord that, if he had spoken as had been reported, he would have been the most shameless liar since he had heard from me the very contrary of what had been represented. He who made the report was utterly confused. However, these intrigues continued apace. . . . Hence I endeavoured as best I could to stop the evil from spreading further. When I called before me those who had been inveigled into this wild project, each one denied it. Nevertheless they marched off, protesting all the while that it was to prevent all disturbance.

After the conspiracy of Amboise, the prince of Condé was imprisoned and prosecuted for treason. The *parlement* of Paris pronounced a sentence of death against him on 26 November 1560. Nine days later, before the sentence had been carried out, Francis II died and was succeeded by his even younger brother, Charles IX. Calvin saw the hand of providence in the death of Francis but was rightly alarmed at the naïve optimism which overcame his co-religionists. He advised them instead to work for a limited but secure degree of toleration for their religious worship.

In the meantime, he wrote a memorandum of advice for the vacillating Henry of Navarre. It was the closest that the Genevan reformer came to direct interference in the political affairs of France. The first requisite, he told Navarre, was the release of the prince of Condé and a declaration of his innocence. But the key to the future security of the Protestants lay in a proper council of regency, appointed by the estates general (which had just begun its deliberations at Orléans on 10 December 1560). Calvin also hoped that a process of national petitioning of the estates by the Protestants would result in the removal of the persecution of the faithful.

In fact, no such council of regency was established and, instead, the queen mother, Catherine de Medici, established herself as regent. In due course, she organized a conference, or colloquy, at Poissy in September 1561, which was attended by theologians and spokesmen from both religions. Calvin mistrusted the conference, fearing that it was a device to divide the reformed community in France. He corresponded regularly with the head of the reformed delegation there, Theodore Beza, and was greatly relieved when he heard that it had broken up without achieving anything.

The queen mother was also responsible for a series of edicts in April, July and October 1561 which granted the Protestants in France some relief from persecution and some limited rights of conscience. These were not enforced by the law courts, especially in Paris and Toulouse, and they merely served, at this late stage, to increase the sectarian tensions in French cities until the civil war erupted in May 1562. During the first period of civil war (1562-3) Calvin's influence was limited to that of a largely powerless spectator. He tried to prevent the soldiers, led by the aggressive Protestant military captain in Lyons, François de Beaumont, baron des Adrets, from pillaging Church property in the one major city which fell to the Protestants. He also played a part in the raising of cash for the mercenary soldiers levied in

Germany under d'Andelot, Coligny's brother. The pacification on 19 March 1563 came as a grave disappointment to Calvin, who regarded it as a piece of disgraceful treachery to the Protestant cause on the part of the prince of Condé.

167   Memorandum to Henry of Navarre (undated – c. December 1560)

The second point is the principal one, because upon it everything else depends. It is to establish a regency council. If the king does not show a great deal of firmness at the very outset in this matter, there is a danger that his fault may prove irreparable. To consent to a widow, a foreigner and an Italian [Catherine de Medici] having the principal authority would not only turn out very much to his great discredit, but would also prove so prejudicial to the crown that he will always be blamed for it. To grant her as many honours as possible will not hinder him from retaining the highest ranks for himself. But however he acts in this respect, it is absolutely essential to insist upon the establishment of a council, which can only be done in the estates. The king is well aware that it would not be prudent to go about the business in any other way, and even if the council could be established without their assistance, the precedent would be a bad one. . . .

The third point concerns the religious question. . . . If our petitions are accepted, the least thing we can surely expect from them is that they will procure us a bare and grudging provision by which persecution will be ended for those who do not seek to disturb the peace or intend to cause a disturbance. It will suffice that those who cannot with a good conscience attend mass, be permitted to stay away from it; and in order that such persons are not denounced as without any religion, they should be permitted to assemble together to pray and hear the Word of God with express rules and regulations, enforced with strict penalties laying down the prescribed limits upon such permission. In time, this might be relaxed in their favour. Meanwhile, all those who consent to it would be enrolled in the presence of officers and agents of the king in each *parlement* of justice so that some of the senior members of society would act as guarantors for everything.

CR XLVI, cols. 285–7

168   To Theodore Beza (10 September 1561)

Whatever others may think, it has always been my conviction that the boasted results of the conference [at Poissy] would come to nothing. Believe me, the bishops will never proceed to a serious discussion, not that there are not those amongst them who, I do not doubt, are filled with laudable desires and high expectations. But those at the helm would rather be driven to extremes than forced to be moderate by such a method as this.

CR XLVI, cols. 682-3

169   To Ambrose Blaurer (May 1561)

In many cities [in France] the papists have broken out in tumults, not without bloodshed. In Paris they have been twice vigorously repressed and severely manhandled. The court of *parlement* there not only deceives us, but seems to consider it an advantage to kindle animosity against us. Despite that, it is incredible how the kingdom of God is spreading far and wide. From all sides the demands for ministers are addressed to us, and though we have no more to send, yet such is their insistence that we have to choose certain ministers from the lower ranks of the people. The *parlement* of Toulouse is even more atrocious than that of Paris. Many are still in prison there.

CR XLVI, col. 474

170   To the Baron des Adrets (13 May 1562)

. . . More important, you should make every effort . . . and correct one abuse which is altogether intolerable. I allude to the pretensions of the soldiery to have a right to plunder the chalices, reliquaries and other furniture of the temples. What is worse, it has been reported that one of the ministers has so identified himself with these plunderers as to cause some of this booty to be put up for sale. If this is true, it will cause a dreadful scandal and make the gospel be spoken of with malice, and even if the mouths of the wicked are not encouraged to blaspheme the name of God, it is still quite unlawful to touch public property without a public authorization.

CR XLVII, col. 412

171   To the churches of Languedoc (undated – September 1562)

. . . The point in question is to find money to support the troops which M. d'Andelot has levied. This is not the moment to enter into investigations or disputes to find fault with mistakes which have been committed in the past. For whatever may have been their cause, God has reduced us to such an extremity that if we are not succoured from that quarter, we can expect nothing, according to human probability, except a pitiful and horrible desolation. I know well that although all should be ruined and lost, God has incomprehensible means of re-establishing his Church as if he raised it from the dead, and it is that trust in which we must reside and wait with patience. . . . It is certain that laziness and indifference and the meanness of the churches have resulted in greater suffering than it is possible to estimate. Several who have spared a part of their goods have been condemned to lose them all. What is worse, there are an infinite number of poor people who have answered for the rest with their lives through no fault of their own.

CR XLVII, col. 550

172   To Bullinger (8 April 1563)

We have been basely betrayed by the other brother as well [Condé]. He had promised by an oath, which he asked to be printed, that he would conclude nothing without the consent of his associates. . . . The lust for power has entirely blinded the man. Meanwhile he thinks that he has achieved something important because he is enrolled amongst the knights of the royal order, and delights in puerilities of that sort. . . . You see, my worthy brother, what we have been reduced to by the inconstancy of one man; for he might have obtained without any difficulty from the queen whatever conditions he pleased, but he has voluntarily prostituted himself in the basest subservience.

CR XLVII, cols. 690, 693

C Health, Wealth, Family and Friends

Calvin's daily routine was a punishing one and it had begun to affect his health in his early middle age. In 1559 his condition deteriorated and the last edition of the *Institutes* was completed in the shadow of growing physical disabilities, fevers, stomach pains and headaches. By February 1564 Calvin received the advice of the physicians at Montpellier – amongst the best in Europe – but it is clear from his letter of thanks to them that their pains had not been able to mitigate his own. His wife had died in April 1549 and, during thse last years, he was looked after by his brother, Antoine Calvin, and by his friends among the French exiles in Geneva. Although it was frequently claimed by his enemies that Calvin had made himself a wealthy man through his ministry, he regularly repudiated the charge and his will proved his lack of means. Towards the end of his life, he felt keenly the loss of some of his friends in the plague in Geneva in 1560 and missed his fellow-ministers when they were away from the city.

173   Calvin's energy

I do not believe that there can be found his like. Who can recount his ordinary and extraordinary labours? I doubt if any man in our time had more to listen to, to reply to, or to write, about things of greater importance. The multitude and quality alone of his writings is enough to astonish every one who looks at them, and even more those who read them. . . . He never ceased working day and night in the service of the Lord, and heard most unwillingly the prayers and exhortations that his friends addressed to him every day to give himself some rest.

> *CR* XXI, col. 107 (*Life of Calvin* by Nicolas Colladon, one of his fellow ministers)

174   To Peter Martyr (2 March 1559)

As to myself, most accomplished sir and respected brother, I have nothing to report, except that the violence of my fever has abated. But my bodily strength and vigour of mind have been so much shattered that I do not yet feel greatly relieved. For I seem even more tired now than when I was struggling against its attacks. The weakness of my stomach is a particular cause of suffering to me, and it is increased by a catarrh which brings a cough with it. The vapours from my indigestion trouble my brain and, in turn, my lungs. To all this has been added for the last week some painful haemorrhoids which are often called blind ones because you cannot force the blood from them. If anything is to be relied on from the seasons of the year, my sole remaining hope lies in spring.

CR XLV, col. 468

175   To Nicholas des Gallars (3 October 1560)

Nicholas des Gallars was a Genevan preacher, much respected by Calvin, who was sent to London in 1560 to reorganize the strangers' church there after the accession of Elizabeth I.

Diseases have raged amongst our townspeople since your departure. Two of them are dead – Tagaut and Gaspard – and even that most excellent individual Macard has been taken away from us, to universal sorrow.[2] You can well imagine from my disposition how bitterly I have felt so many bereavements. Baduel drags me on as well as he can and Bernard and Chevalier have got rid of their fever.[3] Colic, inflammation of the lungs and a fever have severely tried me. Though we have a great deficiency of ministers, yet our brethren have, up till now, consistently postponed electing your successor. . . . Beza's absence, besides putting an extraordinary burden of preaching upon me, is an irritant for many other reasons. It distresses me that our worthy brother should be persistently beset with dangers, and I see little prospect of his return. It torments me cruelly to reflect how, urged on by necessity, we have not hesitated to imperil the life of so singular a friend and so excellent a man.[4] Other secret griefs I keep shut up in my heart. Farewell most worthy brother.

CR XLVI, col. 214

[2] Jean Tagaut, born in Amiens, professor of philosophy and mathematics in Lausanne and, from 1559, in Geneva. Jean Macard, from Provence, studied in Paris and withdrew to Geneva in 1548. He was elected a minister in 1556 and briefly served in Paris in 1558. Gaspard was probably one of the Genevan ministers.

[3] Claude Baduel had established the academy of Nîmes and was a minister in Geneva. Bernard and Chevalier cannot be identified.

[4] Beza was absent on a dangerous mission to the king of Navarre. The affair at Amboise had not put an end to plotting. A partial uprising had been planned for September 1560 with Navarre at its head. Calvin even organized the collecting of funds for it. At the last moment, Navarre demanded its postponement. These were the 'secret griefs' that Calvin refers to.

176   To Theodore Beza (27 August 1561)

I am obliged to dictate this letter to you from my bed, and in the deepest affliction from the loss of my dear friend De Varennes who has hitherto been my principal staff and comfort in all my troubles.[5] The great consolation to me in my sorrow is that nothing could have been more peaceful than the manner of his death, which he seemed to invite with outstretched arms as cheerfully as if it had been some delicious enjoyment.

CR XLVI, col. 648

177   To the physicians of Montpellier (8 February 1564)

Twenty years ago I experienced the same courteous services from the distinguished physicians in Paris . . . but then I was not attacked by arthritis, knew nothing of the stone or gravel, was not troubled with chronic indigestion, or afflicted with haemorrhoids, nor yet threatened by the coughing up of blood. At present all these ailments, as it were, muster in troops against me.

CR XLVIII, col. 253

D Calvin's Death

On Friday 28 April 1564 Calvin called the congregation of ministers to his bedside and bade them farewell. His words were taken down afterwards from memory by the minister Jean Pinant. They are the voice of a determined, but exhausted man. In fact, he lived a few more weeks and died on 27 May. He was buried the following day without a tombstone, as he himself had wished. On 2 June 1564 all the ministers and professors in the Genevan academy and Church assembled, and Beza spoke of the loss which the Church and city had experienced. Beza later put on paper his more intimate memories of Calvin, his qualities as a theologian and his personality, very different from the austere, humourless and unapproachable figure that has come down to us.

[5] Guillaume de Trie, sieur de Varennes, one of the senior members of the French exiles in Geneva. He arrived there from Lyons in 1549 and became an intimate friend to Calvin and his neighbour in the rue des chanoines. *See above*, p. 103.

178   Calvin's farewell to the congregation of ministers

It may be thought that I am too hasty in concluding that my end is
drawing near; and that I am not so ill as I think; but I assure you that,
though I have often felt very ill, I have never felt myself in such a state,
nor so weak as I am now. When they take me to put me to bed, my head
fails me and I lose consciousness straight away. There is also this
shortness of breath which oppresses me more and more. I seem to be
different from other sick people who, when death approaches, their
senses fail and they become delirious. In my case, whilst it is true that I
feel paralysed, yet it seems that God is concentrating all my senses
within me, and I believe that I shall have great difficulty and it will cost
me a huge effort to die. . . .

When I first came to this Church, I found almost nothing in it.
There was preaching, and that was all. They would hunt out idols, it is
true, and they would burn them. But there was no reformation. Everything was in disorder. . . .

I have lived here amidst continual bickerings. I have been saluted in
derision of an evening before my door with 40 or 50 shots from
arquebuses. I am, and always have been, a poor and timid scholar, so
you can imagine how much that astonished me. Then afterwards I was
expelled and went away to Strasbourg, and when I had spent some
time there I was called back here again, but I had the same difficulty in
the carrying out of my duties as before. They set dogs at my heels
crying, 'At him, at him!' and these snapped at my gown and legs. I
went to the 'council of 200' when they were fighting, and I kept back
others who wanted to go and had no business to be there. And though
there are some who boast that they did everything . . . yet I was there,
and, as I entered, people said to me, 'Withdraw, sir, we have nothing
to say to you!' I replied, 'I will do no such thing – come, come, wicked
men that you are; kill me and my blood will rise against you and these
very benches will require it so'. Thus I have had conflicts, and you will
experience others no less but even greater. You are in a perverse and
unhappy nation, and though there are good men in it, the nation is
perverse and wicked, and you will have troubles when God calls me
away. For though I am nothing, yet I know well that I have prevented
3,000 tumults which might have occurred in Geneva. But take
courage, and fortify yourselves, for God will make use of this Church
and will maintain it and assures you that he will protect it.

I have had many infirmities which you have been obliged to bear with, and what is more, all I have done is worthless. The ungodly will seize on that, but I repeat that all I have done has been worthless and that I am a miserable creature. But certainly I may say this, that I have meant for the best, that my vices have always displeased me, and that the root of the fear of the Lord has always been in my heart. You may say 'he meant well' and I pray that my evil may be forgiven and that if there was anything good you may confirm yourselves by it and have it as an example.

[Calvin ended with further pieces of advice and then] He took his leave courteously of all the brethren one by one, shaking them by the hand, all melting into tears. Written the last day of May 1564, on the 27th day of which month he died.

CR XXXVII, cols. 890–4

179   Epitaph from the consistory in Geneva

As concerns the late M. Calvin who had been like a father in the midst of our society and the same to each one of us individually. God had given him such qualities and had accompanied this by such authority over the people which he used to help each of us to serve the better in our ministry so that if we had needed to make an appointment every year we could not have selected any one else from our society: to have done otherwise would have been to ignore the amazing and great qualities that God had bestowed on Calvin; joined to those was a sincerity and conscientiousness which all could perceive. And in truth God had so blessed his conduct that in every sphere, including all that concerned our ministry, our society never lacked good and sensible advice, and it was always obvious that he never thought about his own advantage or that of his relatives but treated every one alike.

Registres II, p. 103

180   Beza's recollections of John Calvin

He was of moderate stature, of a pale and dusky complexion with eyes that sparkled to the moment of his death and bespoke his great intellect. In dress he was neither over-fastidious nor mean, but such as became his singular modesty. In diet he was temperate, being equally averse to abstinence and indulgence. He was most sparing in the qualities of his food, and for many years took only one meal a day on account of his weak stomach. He took little sleep, and had such an astonishing memory that any person whom he had seen once, he instantly recognized again at a distance of years; and when, in the course of dictating, he happened to be interrupted for several hours, as often happened, as soon as he returned he began again where he had left off. . . .

On whatever subject he was consulted his judgement was so clear and correct that he often seemed to prophesy; nor do I remember any person being led astray in consequence of following his advice. He despised mere eloquence and was sparing in his use of words, but he was by no means a careless writer. No theologian of this period . . . wrote more purely, weightily and judiciously, though he wrote more than any one else, either in our recollection or that of our fathers. For, by the hard studies of his youth and a certain acuteness of judgement, confirmed by practice at dictation, he was never at a loss for an appropriate and weighty expression and wrote very much as he spoke. In the doctrine which he delivered at first, he persisted through to the end, scarcely making any changes. That could not be said of many theologians of our time. . . .

Although nature had formed him to be serious, yet, in the common affairs of life, there was no man more pleasant to deal with. In bearing with infirmities he was patient; he never made the weaker brethren blush, or terrified them by an intemperate rebuke, yet he never connived at or flattered their faults. He was as determined and severe an enemy of adulation, dissimulation and dishonesty (especially where religion was concerned) as he was a lover of truth, simplicity and candour. He was naturally of a sharp temper, and this had been increased by the strenuous life he had led. But the Spirit of the Lord had so taught him to command his anger that no word was heard to proceed from him unbecoming a good man.

CR XLIX, cols. 169–70

Epilogue

Neither Calvin's stature as a theologian nor the existence of a Calvinist Church in various parts of Europe could prevent his work becoming the subject of interpretation and reassessment. There is a world of difference between what Calvin said and what later Calvinists interpreted him as saying. A generation of theologians after his death made his work more legalistic, presbyterian and predestinarian in its emphases, culminating in the famous Synod at Dort in the Netherlands where one of the propositions stated that Calvinists believed that Christ had died only for the elect. Seventeenth-century moralists stressed vocation, eighteenth-century industrialists the work ethic. It is a tribute to Calvin's thought that it was flexible in its freedom of application to a constantly changing world.

Persecution of Calvinists and suspicion of Calvinist beliefs created a series of 'diasporas' in Europe and these profoundly influenced the nature of Calvinism as well. Calvinists were expelled from Bohemia in 1620 and from France officially in 1685. They had already been removed from Flanders in the 1580s and they felt uncomfortable in England in the years of the Laudian reaction (the 1630s). The 'diaspora' is one reason why Calvinism became strongly implanted in the New World. It is impossible to understand the Massachusetts of John Winthrop, Cotton Mather or Benjamin Franklin without a knowledge of Calvinism in its various historical modes. The Cape Colony of Paul Kruger was indelibly marked by the Calvinism of his seventeenth-century Dutch predecessors; so was Canada by the presbyterianism of its Scottish and Irish immigrants. The influence of Calvinism in world history has been pervasive and enduring.

Further reading

Exhaustive bibliographies of recent additions to literature concerning Calvin in all languages are to be found for the period 1901–59 in W. Niesel, *Calvin-Bibliographie (1901-1959)* (Munich, 1961) and for the following decade in J.N. Tylenda, *Calvin Bibliography (1960-1970)* in the *Calvin Theological Journal* VI, no. 2.

Amongst the older biographies, two stand out in quality: E. Doumergue, *Jean Calvin. Les hommes et les choses de son temps* (Lausanne, 7 vols., 1899–1927) and F. Wendel, *Calvin. The Origins and Development of his Religious Thought*, translated by P. Mairet from the French edition of 1950 (London, 1969). The most recent biography in English is T.H.L. Parker, *John Calvin* (London, 1975). In many ways, Theodore Beza's *Life of Calvin* (translated into English by Henry Beveridge in *Tracts and Treatises on the Reformation of the Church* I, Edinburgh, 1844) still captures the flavour of Calvin's life effectively.

Studies of Calvin's writings are numerous. In English, the following works are amongst the most interesting of those published since 1945: T.H.L. Parker, *The Oracles of God. An Introduction to the Preaching of John Calvin* (London, 1947); W. Niesel, *The Theology of Calvin* (translated by H. Knight, London, 1956); F.M. Higman, *The Style of John Calvin in his French Polemical Treatises* (Oxford, 1967); T.H.L. Parker, *Calvin's Doctrine of the Knowledge of God* (Edinburgh, 1969). The economic and social implications of Calvin's writings are exhaustively treated only in A. Biéler, *La Pensée économique et sociale de Calvin* (Geneva, 1959). Calvin's political thought has been extensively reinterpreted in a broader context in volume II of Q. Skinner, *Foundations of Modern Political Thought* (Cambridge, 1978). Useful reassessment is to be anticipated from H. Höpfl, *The Christian Polity of John Calvin* (Cambridge, 1982).

Geneva in the sixteenth century can be explored through the works of E.W. Monter, especially *Calvin's Geneva* (New York, 1967) and also that of A. Perrenoud, *La population de Genève, XVIe-XIXe siècles* (Geneva, 1979).

The wider impact of Calvinism can be approached in many different ways. One unitary approach is to be found in J.T. McNeill, *The History and Character of Calvinism* (New York, 1954). French Protestantism and the edicts of heresy (later, those of toleration) forms the theme of N.M. Sutherland, *The Huguenot Struggle for Recognition* (New Haven, 1980). Parts of J.H.M. Salmon, *Society in Crisis: France in the Sixteenth Century* (London, 1975) and various articles in N.Z. Davis, *Society and Culture in Early Modern France* (Stanford, California, 1975) investigate Calvinist appeal in France. R.M. Kingdon, *Geneva and the Coming of the Wars of Religion in France (1555-1563)* (Geneva, 1956) looks at the recruitment, training and missionary activity of ministers trained in Geneva and sent to France. Amongst the recent biographies, J. Ridley, *John Knox* (Oxford, 1968) and Jean-François Gilmont, *Jean Crespin, un éditeur réformé du XVIe siècle* (Geneva, 1981) are exemplary. Theodore Beza still awaits a good modern study.